A CURRICULUM DEVELOPMENT HANDBOOK FOR EARLY CHILDHOOD EDUCATORS

A CURRICULUM DEVELOPMENT HANDBOOK FOR EARLY CHILDHOOD EDUCATORS

Edited by Iram Siraj-Blatchford

Trentham Books

First published in 1998 by Trentham Books Limited

Trentham Books Limited
Westview House
734 London Road
Oakhill
Stoke on Trent
Staffordshire
England ST4 5NP

British Cataloguing in Publication Data

A catalogue record for this book is available from the British Library

ISBN 1 85856 100 0
ISBN 1 85856 111 6 (hb)

Designed and typeset by Trentham Print Design Ltd., Chester and printed in Great Britain by The Cromwell Press Ltd., Wiltshire

CONTENTS

About the contributors • vii

Introduction
Iram Siraj-Blatchford • ix

PART I: QUALITY

Chapter 1
**Criteria for Determining Quality in Early Learning
for 3-6 year-olds** • 3
Iram Siraj-Blatchford

Chapter 2
The Relationship between Planning and Assessment • 15
Julie Fisher

PART II: CORE LEARNING EXPERIENCES

Chapter 3
**Curiosity and Communication:
Language and Literacy in the Early Years** • 45
Jeni Riley

Chapter 4
Doing Mathematics with Young Children • 61
Patti Barber

Chapter 5
Science in the Early Years • 77
Esmé Glauert

Chapter 6

Physical Development in the Early Years • 93

Pauline Wetton

Chapter 7

**Design, Technology and the use of Computers
in the Early Years** • 109

John Siraj-Blatchford

Chapter 8

**Humanities: Developing a Sense of Place and Time
in the Early Years** • 121

Caroline Heal and John Cook

PART III: CROSS-CURRICULAR LEARNING

Chapter 9

Fostering Creative Development • 139

Bernadette Duffy

Chapter 10

**Thinking about Me and Them:
personal and social development** • 155

Rosemary Roberts

Index • 175

ABOUT THE CONTRIBUTORS

Patti Barber is Lecturer in Primary Education at University of London, Institute of Education. She trained at Homerton College, University of Cambridge and the Institute of Education, University of London 1991-94 where she undertook an MA in Primary Education and Mathematics Education. She has extensive experience of teaching in London schools and as an advisory teacher for maths.

John Cook is Lecturer in Primary Education at University of London, Institute of Education. He was until recently the Deputy Chief Inspector for the London Borough of Tower Hamlets and an Inspector for the Humanities.

Bernadette Duffy is Head of The Dorothy Gardner Early Excellence Centre in Westminster and Chairperson of the National Association of Nursery Centres. She has worked in a wide range of early years' settings over the past twenty years and is committed to the principles of integrated provision and partnership with parents and community. Bernadette is also an NVQ Assessor, Internal Verifier and Nursery Education Inspector. She is co-author of *Great Expectations – a curriculum for the under fives,* published by Westminster LEA, 1996 and co-author of *Supporting Creativity and Imagination in the Early Years*, published by Open University Press, 1998.

Julie Fisher is currently Advisor for Early Years in Oxfordshire. She has been head teacher of two urban schools, one a nursery and infant school and the other a first and middle school combined. Following headship she became Lecturer in Early Childhood Education at the University of Reading where she began her research into classroom management in reception classes. She is the author of *Starting from the Child?* published by Open University Press (1995).

Esmé Glauert is Lecturer in Primary Education at University of London, Institute of Education. She spent many years as an infant teacher in inner London schools and was an advisory teacher for science. Before becoming a teacher she worked in a variety of early years' settings. She has extensive experience of running inservice training for early years practitioners and is an active member of the Association for Science Education.

Caroline Heal is Lecturer in Primary Education at University of London, Institute of Education with a special interest in the Humanities. She has been involved in curriculum development in the Humanities across primary and secondary schools over many years and in particular in the preparation of new teachers committed to developing work in these areas.

Jeni Riley is Head of Primary Education at University of London, Institute of Education and is responsible for the Early Years Course within the Primary PGCE. She teaches on Language and Literacy courses at the Primary PGCE, MA and inservice levels and is involved with research projects on the teaching of literacy in early years' classrooms. She is the author of *The Teaching of Reading: The Development of Literacy in the Early Years of School*, (1996) by Paul Chapman.

Rosemary Roberts is Co-director of Peers Early Education Partnership (PEEP), a project that works with the parents and other important adults of all children aged 0-5 in a disadvantaged area of Oxford about their children's learning at home, from birth. She was formerly head teacher of a LEA nursery school and has taught children throughout the primary age-range, as well as lecturing in higher education. Her writing is informed by the Oxford Tavistock Clinic course in psycho-analytic observational studies.

Iram Siraj-Blatchford is Senior Lecturer in Early Childhood Education (ECE) at University of London, Institute of Education, teaching on postgraduate courses and supervising research students. She has been a teacher in primary and nursery classes and is a governor at a nursery and primary school. She has lectured and published widely on ECE, equal opportunities and research methods. Her books include the *Early Years: Laying the Foundations for Racial Equality* (1994, Trentham Books), *Educating the Whole Child* (1995, Open University Press, edited with John Siraj-Blatchford) and *A Sociology of Educating* (1997, 3rd Edition with Roland Meighan, Cassell). Her most recent book with Viv Moriarty is *An Introduction to Curriculum Development for 3-5 year-olds* published by Education Now, 1998. Iram is co-director of the Effective Provision for Pre-school Education (EPPE) Project funded by the DfEE (1997-2003).

John Siraj-Blatchford is Lecturer in Science Education at the University of Durham, School of Education. He currently teaches science to PGCE students and runs several modules for the BA in Childhood Studies. He has specialised in the field of Science, Design and Technology and is the author of several books, including *Learning Technology, Science and Social Justice* (1996) published by Education Now and co-author of *Teaching and Learning in Further and Higher Education* (1997) published by Falmer Press. His current research includes Technology projects in schools in the UK and Europe and exploring the historical, philosophical and sociological links between science, technology and society.

Pauline Wetton is Lecturer in Education at the University of Durham, School of Education. She is a specialist in the field of Physical Education in the Early Years (3-7). She teaches on both the undergraduate and postgraduate programmes and leads INSET courses for teachers. She has given papers at international conferences and key lectures at various national conferences. Her publications include *Physical Education in the Nursery and Infant School* (1988) Routledge and *Physical Education in the Early Years* (1997) also by Routledge.

INTRODUCTION

This book will be of interest to anyone that is working or intending to work with children in the 3-6 year-old age group. The book draws on the extensive knowledge of staff involved in Early Childhood Education (ECE) courses at the Institute of Education, University of London. Chapters have also been invited from experts in other universities and advisors and headteachers in early childhood education. The book is rooted in our practical experience of young children's learning and the curriculum, and our writing has integrated research and theory in subject areas with what we know about children's learning. Each chapter ends with notes on further recommended reading and information for further development in the particular curriculum area and offers a comprehensive reference section to current readings.

Part I of the book introduces the reader to the context that is required for quality early learning to take place. My chapter on quality criteria does not define quality in a simple way but argues *the case* for quality through what we know about children's learning and about the contribution adults can make in extending and supporting children's development. The chapter also identifies the *kind* of curriculum we should be aiming for and the place of the Desirable Outcomes for ECE within this context. Julie Fisher, in Chapter 2 gives explicit support on the role of planning and assessment in delivering the curriculum. With her experience as an early years advisor in a large local authority she provides us with tried and tested planning and assessment material that can be implemented in any setting.

Part II of the book focuses on core learning experiences which, integrated with cross-curricular issues, should provide a broad and balanced curriculum. Jeni Riley considers the vital role of literacy, language and communication for young children in today's early childhood settings. The strong emphasis on oracy and literacy is dealt with in light of vital continuity between early years settings within and outside the school. Her chapter supports a carefully structured set of experiences for older children, which will ensure that monolingual and bilingual children acquire English literacy skills within an enjoyable context. In Chapter 4 Patti Barber explains the theory behind children's learning of number and illustrates how adults can extend children's development in all areas of mathematics. She encourages practitioners to take account of the wealth of experience children bring with them from home and to build on it. Similarly Esmé Glauert suggests many activities and experiences which children can encounter to develop their scientific understanding. Both science and mathematics are relatively neglected topics in non-national curriculum classes and these chapters provide examples of good practice as they demonstrate children's reactions and learning from practical experiences.

Physical development is an important part of education for young children and there is some evidence that children who enter school early are more likely to remain inactive for longer periods than children in purpose-built early years settings. Pauline Wetton explains the importance of the place of physical education in the curriculum and provides us with ample examples of the benefits of physical activity for young children. Through an exploration of movement, dance and gymnastics activities she shows how to plan for safe and positive experiences which extend physical strength, suppleness, body awareness and fitness in young children. John Siraj-Blatchford deals with the new area of design and technology for young children, a popular subject with children in their primary years and often referred to as a 'favourite' experience. It used to be called 'craft' but here we learn about the value of designing and the role of evaluating designs in promoting children's ability as reflective thinkers. We are also supported in our understanding of the value and use of computers in the early years classroom; selected resources are reviewed for this purpose. The last chapter in this part develops our understanding of the humanities as a curriculum area for young children. Caroline Heal and John Cook sensitively show how even babies are aware of mapping and how young children gradually develop an understanding of time and space through carefully planned experiences. These chapters all offer much support. The authors convey their enthusiasm for their practice as well as the theories which inform their work with young children.

The final part of the book is dedicated to children's personal and social development and to fostering creativity. These areas are often neglected, even though they are now part of the Desirable Outcomes for Nursery Education. This is mainly because base-line assessment has been introduced in local authorities, which tends, in many areas, to give more prominence to assessing language, science and maths. We caution against this. Bernadette Duffy and Rosemary Roberts provide compelling reasons for personal and social development and describe practices which will help educators to justify and promote this aspect of the early years curriculum. More importantly their chapters illustrate clearly how without these concerns it is quite possible that children would find it difficult to access the rest of the curriculum.

I hope you enjoy reading this book as much as the team of authors enjoyed meeting and talking about it, and writing and discussing it.

PART I

QUALITY

CHAPTER 1

CRITERIA FOR DETERMINING QUALITY IN EARLY LEARNING FOR 3-6 YEAR-OLDS

Iram Siraj-Blatchford

A framework for the curriculum

This book is about extending good practice in curriculum development and supporting and sustaining the positive practices that characterise many early childhood settings. The curriculum cannot be seen in isolation and it cannot exist without a strong and well-developed framework of support, the social and institutional context in which curriculum 'happens'. To develop and deliver a sound curriculum the staff must be well informed about child development and culture and about subject knowledge and appropriate ways of 'teaching' young children so that all the children in their setting can access the curriculum. Time needs to be spent developing shared perspectives so that everyone is pulling in the same direction.

Staff need time to develop a shared understanding of children, curriculum, learning and the role of adults in supporting learning. Research on school improvement and effectiveness suggests that where staff had been involved in the development of guidelines for their school, there was likely to be school-wide consistency in guideline usage. Where staff had not been involved, however, there was likely to be variation, with school teachers (educators) tending to adopt individual approaches to the use of guidelines for different curriculum areas. Staff involvement seems to be related to a consistent school-based approach to curriculum (Mortimore *et al*, 1988). In my own research on settings, which deliberately incorporated a care and education philosophy, it appeared to be important that staff working towards a quality curriculum pursued common understanding of:

Curriculum knowledge
Active learning through scaffolding and play
Equal opportunities
Family and community partnerships
Primary educators/key persons
Interactions with adults and peers
Assessment, observation and record keeping
Staff development
Environment factors (resource constraints)
Multi-disciplinary teams
Management matters
(Siraj-Blatchford, 1995)

From time to time each of these aspects will need to be systematically reviewed if a shared philosophy among staff is to be developed. Many of these issues are dealt with more fully in the chapters that follow; for example, Chapter 2 deals in detail with planning and assessment. In this chapter, following a discussion of curriculum content I discuss the role of parents in supporting their children's learning. I focus upon the process of learning for young children and how educators can successfully support children in their learning.

A Desirable Outcomes *Plus* Curriculum

The Rumbold Report (1990) emphasised the importance of a balanced approach to knowledge and learning, based on those purposes previously identified in HMI publications on the education of 5-16 year-olds. It emphasised a balance between concepts, knowledge and understanding, attitudes and skills, within a framework based on subjects, resource areas, broad themes or areas of learning. The Rumbold framework also followed that outlined in the 1985 HMI discussion document (*The Curriculum 5 to 16*) and included the following areas of experience and learning:

Aesthetic and creative
Human and social
Linguistic and literary
Mathematical
Physical
Scientific
Technological
Moral and spiritual

To this list we can now add:

Success, self-esteem and resilience
Cultural identity

Success, self-esteem and resilience was added to this list by Kathy Sylva in the START RIGHT Report (1994) in response to research by Dweck and Leggett (1988) in the United States. The research emphasised the importance of 'mastery' learning dispositions in children's educational development. There is evidence that children who experience education through taking some responsibility for their actions and learning become more effective learners. They are learning not only the content of the curriculum but the processes by which learning takes place. In the final chapter of this book, Rosemary Roberts treats the important area of personal and social education as a curriculum area worthy of separate activities, planning and assessment.

Cultural identity has also been added to the above list and this is seen as a significant area of concern for curriculum development (Siraj-Blatchford, 1996). All children and adults identify with classed, gendered and racialised groups (as well as other groups) but what is especially significant is that some cultural identities are seen as less 'academic' than others (often by the staff and children). We already know that children can hold views about their 'masterful' or 'helpless' attributes as learners (Dweck and Leggett, 1988).

These views tend to be subject related and lead to underachievement in some areas of the curriculum. Children construct their identities in association with their perceived cultural heritage (Siraj-Blatchford, 1996). Recently we have heard a good deal in the press about boys' underachievement and certainly the results from the school league-tables suggest that some boys do underachieve in terms of basic literacy, but it is important to note that this is only certain groups of boys and not all boys. Working-class white boys and African-Caribbean boys are particularly vulnerable. Similarly, children from some ethnic minority groups perform poorly in significant areas of the curriculum while other ethnic minority groups achieve particularly highly (Gillborn and Gipps, 1997).

It is apparent that certain confounding identities, for instance, white/working class/male, can lead to lower outcomes because of expectations held by the children and adults. In asserting their masculinity, white working-class boys might choose gross-motor construction activities over reading or pre-reading activities. Similarly, some girls may identify more strongly with home-corner play and favour nurturing activities over construction choices. Class, gender and ethnicity are complicit here and the permutations are not simple but they do exist and do lead to underachievement. Educators need to take an active role in planning for, supporting and developing individual children's identities as competent learners of a broad and balanced curriculum.

In the active construction of their identities, children distance themselves from 'others' (Siraj-Blatchford, Iram and John, 1998). The issue is therefore to show children that they are mistaken in associating these 'others' with particular areas of the curriculum. We have to extend children's identity as learners and break down the stereotypes. Boys need to disassociate literacy from 'girls' stuff, and be presented with strong masculine role models that value literacy. It is in this context that we can see the benefits of the current Government's new pilot scheme developed with the football Premier League. In partnership with the Government, local authorities and football clubs, study support centres are being established at Premier League grounds for the benefit of local children.

In contrast to the comprehensive list of subjects and cross-curricular dimensions listed above, the recent *Nursery Education: Desirable Outcomes for Children's Learning on Entering Compulsory Education* (SCAA/DfEE, 1996) includes only six areas of development:

> Personal and Social Development
> Language and Literacy
> Mathematics
> Knowledge and Understanding of the World
> Physical Development
> Creative Development

This is a limited and limiting curriculum, but probably necessary given that the curriculum was introduced because the Government wanted to improve educational standards. Although this may sound contradictory, it is not. If standards are to be improved they need to be measured in some way, and some areas of the curriculum lend themselves to measurement more than others. Unfortunately, the variation in training of early childhood educators, the combination of market-led provision of voluntary, private and state services and the lack of co-ordination between them has left us with uneven educational standards.

The rationale behind the Desirable Outcomes is to set a 'base-line' educational standard. In principle this should be applauded, and it is to be hoped that settings where training opportunities and resources have been poor will begin to raise their standards. At the same time no setting should feel strait-jacketed by the *Outcomes* curriculum. Many early childhood settings from a variety of provisions are already delivering a richer and more complex curriculum than that outlined and implied in the Desirable Outcomes. It is essential that we hold on to the wider picture of curriculum quality and see the 'desirable outcomes' for what they are – an instrumental and limited base-line.

In this book we support the inclusion of all aspects of the former HMI curriculum with the addition of the two cross-curricular dimensions mentioned above. We therefore incorporate the Desirable Outcomes guidance for four year-olds. The curriculum presented here provides a more robust Desirable Outcomes *Plus* guidance to the curriculum that more closely reflects the depth and variety of good practice found in many settings. The fact that it is aimed at 3-6 year-olds means that the early stage of the National Curriculum is taken into account.

Cross-curricular themes such as personal and social education and gender equity have been recognised as significant curriculum initiatives in the development of all children (Siraj-Blatchford, John and Iram, 1995). In the early years curriculum the Schools Curriculum and Assessment Authority had asserted that the Desirable Outcomes can deliver these:

> 'Taken together, the six areas of learning also provide opportunities to address important aspects of children's spiritual, moral, social and cultural development'. (SCAA, 1996 p.4)

These areas are not a strength in many settings and their implementation requires a commitment to the development of equality of opportunity. It is imperative that we provide an environment that is welcoming, happy, safe and secure and that reflects the community it serves. The environment should be free from negative messages that are damaging to any individual regardless of their race, religion, language or culture (Clarke and Siraj-Blatchford, 1994).

The curriculum should offer a range of appropriate *breadth* and *balance* in subject matter and needs to be carefully planned to match children's abilities. Educators will need to ensure that the curriculum has *relevance* to the lives of young children – they often enter a setting assuming we know everything they do! Hence, we are familiar with questions from little children such as: 'You know my goldfish?' Getting to know the child's parents and the child (as described in Chapters 2 and 10) will help us to *differentiate* tasks, experiences and activities which extend each child's development and build on their interests and prior understandings.

Variety and *pace* in the curriculum are an important feature in 'teaching' young children. Due attention should be given to children's ability to concentrate and persevere at particular tasks, and the range of choices in terms of materials and experiences will determine whether children remain motivated or become bored. Continuity and progression are two dimensions which are normally associated with the 'next stage' of education. With young children it is especially important to consider *continuity* and *progression* from the home; I will return to this under the section on the child's 'natural' curriculum. *Active* learning experiences in the context of a *combined* care and education philosophy will support children in their development of feelings as well as educational dimensions.

Parents supporting children's learning

Not only may the experience at home provide something not readily available in school but also it seems that the skills involved apply as much to the process of attention, perseverance, task performance and work organisation as to particular areas of knowledge. Learning how to learn may be as important as the specifics of what is learned. (Rutter, 1985)

The Education Reform Act (DES, 1988) identifies the role of parents as vital to the reform of schools and to the process of raising educational standards through their greater involvement in decision making and the governance of schools. Some research on parent involvement, for instance studies in reading and literacy development (Hewison, 1988; Hannon and James, 1990), suggest that children's educational development can be enhanced with long term positive effects. Researchers have investigated the reasons for poor reading scores among working-class children and some minority ethnic groups so that they can be improved.

Studies prior to the 1980s suggested that home background based on factors such as socio-economic advantage, parent attitudes and family size did relate to a child's achievement in reading scores. Hewison and Tizard (1980) studied a cohort of working-class children to find out which factors made the greatest difference in determining whether a child would learn to read. Whether the mother heard the child read regularly seemed to be much more important than the mother's competence in language or the child's IQ. Other studies have shown that educators' involvement in the home can make a positive impact on reading (Hannon, 1987) and early learning e.g. the High/Scope Perry Pre-school Study (Schweinhart et al, 1993).

If we accept that parents are their children's first teachers then it is likely to follow that learning outcomes will be more effective where there is some consensus and consistency between the home and the early childhood setting's approach to the child's learning (Jowett *et al.*, 1991; Long, 1992;

Epstein, 1988; 1991; Schaeffer, 1992). Positive partnerships with parents can be achieved when there is honesty and mutual respect and where we, as educators, develop strategies for sharing and show a willingness to negotiate. Educators must take the responsibility for building confidence and getting to know parents as people with a background and views which affect their everyday actions.

There are a number of reasons why it is important to involve parents in the daily life of an early years setting. Each child is an individual. Their language and culture shape their development. Parents can provide valuable information and insights about their children. Regular discussions with parents assist staff to become better informed about the child's needs. Parents have a contribution to make in planning the curriculum and might a significant contribution in working towards common goals for their children. The way we respond to parents deserves the same attention and effort as work with children. Each parent is an individual and their first priority is to their own child so it is unreasonable to restrict their involvement to supporting the whole group. Yet this is often the only condition on which educators accept their help.

Engaging with the child's 'natural curriculum'

Young children enter educational institutions with a great deal of knowledge and skills already in place. They have learnt many things at home and in their community environment. All children will have established their own patterns of learning which are developed during their 'natural' day-to-day experiences. We could call this their 'natural curriculum', a unique and ad-hoc programme they followed before entering pre-school. However, the processes by which children will have acquired this knowledge of the world around them will be very similar to the ones advocated in this book.

The key processes of learning will have been through play, watching adults and other children perform tasks, by partaking in real-life experiences and through talking about these experiences with others. Children enter the educational setting with a wealth of preferences and prejudices, and with knowledge and experiences associated with language, maths, science, technology and sociability plus other skills and information. The way children articulate and reflect upon this knowledge and experience will depend on the expectations held by those around them. In the home environment most children will have had (and continue to have) a rich experience embedded within cultural meanings that are familiar to them (Tizard and Hughes, 1984). How can the early childhood educators, whether in the context of a playgroup or a primary school classroom, build upon this learning?

The process of learning

For effective curriculum implementation in early childhood education (ECE) the context in which learning takes place needs to be highlighted. The importance of clear aims, careful planning, curriculum integration, and the centrality of play and interactions, has to be considered alongside the role of the adults, a strong partnership with parents, continuity and progression, observation, assessment and recording and the review cycle. The Rumbold report sets out another prerequisite for learning:

> For the early years educator – how children are encouraged to learn – is as important as, and inseparable from, the content – what they learn. We believe that this principle must underlie all curriculum planning....

> ... educators should guard against pressures which might lead them to over-concentration on formal teaching and upon the attainment of a specific set of targets.

The understanding of learning underpinning this chapter is based upon principles of social constructivism drawn from both Vygotsky and Piaget but also conditioned by a cautious scepticism regarding any alleged *essential* or *natural* limitations to children's intellectual development. What this means in practice is that I accept Piaget's account of 'intellectual adaptation' as the most convincing model that has yet been put forward. Piaget describes a learning mechanism which involves children in the active elaboration of their own mental structures as they assimilate and accommodate new experiences. For Piaget, this learning machine was 'fuelled' by the affect of 'interest' and triggered by any form of 'disequilibrium' between experience and the child's prior knowledge and skill. Piaget also argued that the child's intellectual adaptation was as much an adaptation to the *social* environment as it was an adaptation to the physical and material environment. This provides a strong foundation for early years educational practice as it accounts simultaneously for learning and for motivation.

This latter part of his theory, which provides an account of the role of social factors in early childhood development has, unfortunately, been relatively neglected (DeVries, 1997). Piaget argued that adult-child relations influence every aspect of development and that affective and personality development are intimately related to intellectual and moral development. Perhaps most importantly, Piaget argued that reciprocity in peer relations provide the foundations for perspective taking and decentering. This suggests that *colla-borative* play is exceptionally important for children. According to DeVries, Piaget proposed ways in which co-operative social interaction between children and between children and adults function to promote cognitive, affective and moral development and as she says:

> If Piaget was correct, then we need to reconsider the structure and methods of our schools from the point of view of long term effects on children's sociomoral, affective and intellectual development. (p16 *op cit*)

It is to Vygotsky that we are indebted for the foundations of our theories of teaching 'as assisted performance' (Tharp and Gallimore, 1991). Vygotsky defined what he referred to as the 'zone of proximal development' (ZPD) as:

> ...the distance between the actual developmental level as determined by individual problem solving and the level of potential development as determined through problem solving under adult guidance or in collaboration with more capable peers. (Vygotsky, 1978, p86)

The notion has now been popularly extended beyond problem solving to encompass performance in other areas of competence. The aims of teaching, from this perspective, are to assist children within this zone, providing the support and encouragement they require to perform successfully in areas that would otherwise be beyond them. The key challenge for educators becomes one of defining the limits of the zone, matching, or 'tuning' the support, or 'scaffolding' (Wood, Bruner and Ross, 1976), just beyond each child's current independent capabilities. Assistance within children's existing capability is wasted, while assistance beyond the limitations of the zone will be meaningless and potentially damaging to their self-confidence.

As DeVries argues, a great deal of work remains to be done to integrate Piagetian and Vygotskian theory but there can be little doubt that this is worth doing.

Putting together this book, the authors have shared the view that an appropriate curriculum for young children will be one determined with the needs and characteristics of individual and specific groups of children in mind. In adopting the social constructivist approach we are indicating our belief that children learn best when they are being supported by the adult or their peers in developing their individual capability. We also believe that children should be made aware of their learning and of the benefits to be gained from developing their experience in interaction with others. We therefore argue that the early years curriculum should be appropriate to young children's limited experience and to their current social and physiological development. But we also agree with Jerome Bruner that 'anything can be taught to any child in an intellectually honest way' so are cautious about any kind of inherent 'developmental' approach that emphasises what it is that children 'ought to be able to do' at a particular age or stage. Where this approach is adopted, those children who 'fail' to meet the criteria are often considered deficient in some way. Given the variety of experiences that young children bring with them in the early years, we regard these approaches as particularly inappropriate. We would therefore support educators in constructing an environment based on the view that children are active learners and in following the principles below:

Principles of active learning

- Provide children with experiential activities to assist learning of the curriculum

- Activities should be planned for particular groups of children (language, age, ability)

- Encourage and develop co-operative learning

- Stimulate problem solving based on direct observation of the local environment

- Work co-operatively with the parents and community

- Observe and assess the range of learning

- Develop social responsibility in children through classroom structure and negotiated rules

- Create an organised, attractive and exciting class environment

Adapted from Sylva and Siraj-Blatchford (1995)

In addition, any curriculum has to be well planned and based on sound, constructivist practice and delivered by adults who have themselves received sustained, high quality education (Philips, McCartney and Scarr, 1987). The Desirable Outcomes document is a guide to a baseline, so practitioners need not feel restricted as to the depth and content of the curriculum. Nor does it prescribe how practitioners should teach.

Recommended reading:

Moriarty, V. and Siraj-Blatchford, I. (1998) *An Introduction to Curriculum Development for 3-5 year-olds*, Nottingham: Education Now. This book is concerned with practitioners' responses to the Desirable Outcomes and argues for an integrated ECE service which combines care and education philosophies. Short and easy to read, it highlights good practice in key areas of the curriculum and parent involvement for any setting which considers itself as providing a curriculum for children under five.

The Early Years Curriculum Group produces some excellent material and the rather dated publication on *The Early Years and the National Curriculum* (1989) has some good advice for those working on curriculum with 3-6 year-olds.

Further details on Research Projects concerned with Quality in ECE in the UK:

Title: Effective Early Learning (EEL) Project
Principal Project Directors: Christine Pascal and Tony Bertram
Address: Worcester College of Higher Education, Henwick Grove, Worcester, WR2 6AT Tel/Fax: 01905 425681

Title: Quality in Diversity (QuiD) Project
Principal Project Director: Vicky Hurst for the Early Childhood Education Forum
Address: Quality in Diversity Project, c/o National Children's Bureau, 8 Wakley Street, London, EC1V 9QE

Title: Effective Provision of Preschool Education (EPPE) Project
Principal Project Directors: Kathy Sylva, Edward Melhuish, Iram Siraj-Blatchford and Pam Sammons
Address: Child Development and Learning, Institute of Education, University of London, 20 Bedford Way, London. WC1H OAL. Tel: 0171 612 6219. Fax: 0171612 6230.
E-mail: EPPE@ioe.ac.uk

References

Clarke, P. and Siraj-Blatchford, I (1994) 'Working with Bilingual and Multilingual Families', National Children's Bureau Conference, Nottingham Unpublished paper

DES (1988) *The Education Reform Act* London: HMSO

Department for Education and Science, (1990) *Starting with Quality: A report of the committee of enquiry into the quality of educational experiences offered to 3-4 year-olds* (The Rumbold Report) London: HMSO

DeVries, R. (1997) Piaget's Social Theory, *Educational Researcher*, Vol. 26, No. 2 March

Dweck, C. S. and Leggett, E. (1988) 'A social-cognitive approach to motivation and personality', *Psychological Review*, 95, 2, pp. 256-273

Epstein, J. (1988) 'Effective Schools or Effective Students? Dealing with Diversity' in Haskins, R., and MacRae, D. (Eds.) *Policies for America's Public Schools: Teachers, Equity and Indicators.* Norwood, New Jersey: Ablex, pp. 89-126

Epstein, J. L., and Dauber, S.L. (1991) 'School Programs and Teachers Practices of Parent Involvement in Inner-City Elementary and Middle Schools', *The Elementary School Journal*, 91, 3, pp.289-305

Gillborn, D. and Gipps, C. (1997) *Recent Research on the Achievements of Ethnic Minority Pupils* London: HMSO

Hannon, P. and James, A. (1990) Parents' and Teachers' Perspectives on Pre-School Literacy Development', *British Educational Research Journal*, 16, 3

Hannon, P. (1987) A Study of the Effects of Parental Involvement in the Teaching of Reading on Children's reading Test Performance, *British Journal of Educational Psychology*, 57, 56-72

Hewison, J. and Tizard, B. (1980) Parental Involvement and Reading Attainment *British Journal of Educational Psychology*, 50, pp209-215

Hewison, J. (1988) 'The long term effectiveness of parental involvement in reading: a follow-up study to the Haringey reading project', *British Journal of Educational Psychology*, 58, pp.184-190

Jowett, S. and Baginsky, M. (1988) Parents and education: a survey of their involvement and a discussion of some issues, *Educational Research*, 30 (1)

Long, R. (1992) Parent Involvement or Parent Compliance? Parental roles and school improvement, in Mertons *et al Ruling the Margins: Problematising Parent Involvement* London: University of North London

Moriarty, V. and Siraj-Blatchford, I. (1998) *An Introduction to Curriculum Development for 3-5 year-olds*, Nottingham: Education Now

Mortimore, P. Sammons, P. Stoll, L. and Ecob, R. (1988) *School Matters: The Junior Years.* Somerset: Open Books

Philips, D.A., McCartney, K., and Scarr, S. (1987) 'Child Care Quality and Children's Social Development', *Developmental Psychology,* 23, 4, pp.523-543

Rutter, M., Maughan, B., Mortimore, P., and Ouston, J. (1979) *Fifteen Thousand Hours: Secondary Schools and their Effects on Children,* Somerset: Open Books

School Curriculum and Assessment Authority, (1997) *Looking at Children's Learning: Desirable Outcomes for Children's Learning on Entering Compulsory Education*, Middlesex: SCAA

School Curriculum and Assessment Authority, (1996) *Nursery Education: Desirable Outcomes for Children's Learning on Entering Compulsory Education,* London: SCAA and DfEE

Scott, W. (1996) ' Choices in Learning', in Nutbrown, C. *Children's Rights and Early Education*, London: Paul Chapman pp. 34-43

Schweinhart, L.J., Barnes, H.V. and Weikart, D.P. (1993) *Significant Benefits: The High/Scope Perry Preschool Study through Age 27.* Michigan: High/Scope Educational Research Foundation

Shaeffer, S. (1992) 'Collaborating for Educational Change: the role of parents and the community in school improvement', *International Journal of Educational Development.* 12, 4, pp.277-295

Siraj-Blatchford, I. (1995) 'Combined nursery centres: bridging the gap between care and education' in Gammage and Meighan, *The Early Years: The Way Forward* Nottingham: Education Now

Siraj-Blatchford, I. (1996) ' Language, Culture and Difference' in Nutbrown, C. *Children's Rights and Early Education* London: Paul Chapman pp. 23-33

Siraj-Blatchford, I. and Siraj-Blatchford, J. (Eds.) (1995) *Educating the Whole Child: Cross-curricular skills, themes and dimensions in the primary schools* Buckingham: Open University Press

Siraj-Blatchford, I. and Siraj-Blatchford, J. (1998) 'Race, reform and research in UK primary and pre-schools' a Paper presented at the *American Educational Research Association Conference*, San Diego, April 1998

Sylva, K., and Siraj-Blatchford, I. (1995) *The Early Learning Experiences of Children 0-6: Strengthening Primary Education Through Bridging the Gap between Home and School* Paris: UNESCO

Sylva K., in Ball, C. (1994) *START RIGHT: The importance of Early Learning* London: RSA, pp.105-107

Tharp, R. and Gallimore, R. (1991) A Theory of Teaching as assisted Performance, in Light, P., Sheldon, S. and Woodhead, M. (Eds.) (1991) *Learning to Think*, London: Routledge

Tizard, B. and Hughes, M. (1984) *Young Children Learning* London: Fontana

Vygotsky, L. (1978) *Mind in Society: The development of higher psychological processes*, in Cole, M., John-Steiner, V., Schribner, S. and Souberman, E. (Eds. and trans.) Harvard University Press

Wood, Bruner and Ross, (1976) The role of tutoring in problem solving, *Journal of Child Psychology and Psychiatry* 17(2) p 89-100

CHAPTER 2

THE RELATIONSHIP BETWEEN PLANNING AND ASSESSMENT

Julie Fisher

■ Introduction

Effective planning and assessment are mutually dependent. Planning is of most value when it is informed by systematic assessment of what has been learnt and what has been taught and assessment is of most value when it informs what is planned. But which comes first? Assessment is often referred to as though it always follows planning. The adult plans, teaches and then assesses the results of the teaching. Although this cycle is critical, there is an equally important one that begins with assessment. To plan an appropriate curriculum we must find out what children already know and what they need to know next (Roberts, 1995). This chapter is concerned with establishing the principles which underpin the cycle of teaching and learning, and considering the differences between the purpose of assessments which precede planning and those which follow it.

■ Assessment that comes before planning

By the time children begin statutory schooling, they have already developed a 'breathtaking array of competencies' (Gardner, 1993). This achievement deserves recognition – both in terms of celebrating what children already know and can do and appreciating the contribution of those significant adults who have helped to bring this learning about. Not just before starting school, but throughout their educational careers children draw on the huge range of experiences which they have in every aspect of their daily lives (Hutchin, 1996). Children learn as they watch television, as they read, as they observe other children and adults, as they walk through streets and play in the park.

All these experiences provide a wealth of opportunities for children's knowledge and understanding to be far greater than the sum of their planned nursery or school experiences. It is crucial that educators plan a curriculum from the starting point of children's current knowledge and understanding.

There are two ways of establishing what children already know and can do:

By gathering **information** from the following sources:

- talking to parents and carers

- talking to others who have knowledge of the child as a learner and

- looking at any previous records written on the child.

By gathering **evidence** in the following ways:

- observing what the child does

- listening to what the child says and

- collecting outcomes of the child's work e.g. photographs of models, photocopies of mark making, drawings etc.

It is important to distinguish between *information* and *evidence*. Information from others is a crucial part of the assessment process but it is second-hand and, although offering important perspectives, can sometimes be out of date. So it is important to view information alongside the practitioner's own growing evidence of the child's *current* needs. This evidence can only be gathered by working alongside the child. The most informative and reliable evidence is what a child says and does. In the early years children seldom record at a level that demonstrates their knowledge and understanding. Mark-making and writing demonstrate only a child's developmental stage in mark-making and writing. If an educator wants to know what a child understands about weight or sound or pattern, they have to be alongside the child watching and listening.

Sometimes it is possible for the educator to find out what is needed through observation of the planned day. Sometimes it may be necessary to plan a specific task to elicit the level of a child's knowledge or skill. The nature of tasks which are used for assessment prior to the planning of a specific part of the curriculum are different from those which are designed as a result of those initial assessments. They need to be sufficiently open-ended for children to demonstrate the level of their understanding or the degree of their skill. Closed tasks where the outcomes are predictable or too tightly determined will not show the full extent of children's current competence or learning potential. If the purpose of the task is to demonstrate the full range of a child's competence, the task must be suitably flexible. Tasks that are open-ended and that let children explore, investigate, test and try out are the most valuable. They enable the child to work independently of the adult, thus enabling the adult to do a careful observation of the child or group in action.

Who gathers the evidence?

All those who work with children in an educational setting can make observations of children in action and record what they do and say. Those who are not trained as early childhood educators should have a clear set of instructions which set out precisely what that adult is expected to listen or look for. The educator will be clear about the learning intentions of the task and able to identify the behaviours, the skills and the vocabulary which will give evidence of understanding and learning (see Figure 1).

Observations should be dated and a record kept of what the child says and does (see figure 2). It is the job of the educator to analyse these behaviours in order to make judgements about what the child knows and what they need to know next.

The format of the observation sheet should be designed to suit the preferences of the individual educator or the setting. The observation should allow the following to be noted:

Date: ensuring that a child's development is recorded and that progress can be tracked over time

Context: a very brief description to set the child's achievements in context e.g. did they have support? were they working with others? did they struggle?

Observation: capturing what the child actually says and does

Learning analysis: using the educator's professional judgement to identify the precise skills or understandings or knowledge that the child demonstrated in what they did and said.

Action: prompting the educator to fine-tune short-term planning.

What to look and listen for

Assessments should offer a range of information to inform planning. Evidence needs to be gathered over time to ensure that the adult has a rounded picture of the child as a learner. Each observation should have a clear purpose and a clear focus – otherwise it is possible to watch everything and see nothing. Observation over time will ensure that the full potential of the child is observed. The focus for observation may include the following:

LSA/Parent Helper support sheet

date_____ name of adult _____

class/group/individual _____

activity

intended learning outcomes (concepts/skills/knowledge/attitudes as appropriate)

♦

♦

♦

♦

points for observation (linked to intended learning)

♦

♦

♦

♦

observations

Figure 1: LSA/Parent planning sheet

OBSERVATION RECORD SHEET

Name		Date of Birth	
Date	Time	Length of observation	minutes

Evaluation/Action

Date	Time	Length of observation	minutes

Evaluation/Action

Figure 2: Example observation record sheet

- what vocabulary does the child use?

- what skills does the child demonstrate?

- what knowledge and understanding does the child reveal?

- does the child have misunderstandings about things?

- what approaches to learning does the child use?

- what attitudes to learning does the child have?

- what preferences and interests does the child reveal?

Observations should be in all areas of learning, during both teacher-initiated and child-initiated learning and when children are working together or alone.

Finding time for observations and conversations

Time has to be planned to watch and listen to children. The following sheet was designed by a teacher who wanted to raise the status of observation in her classroom and who recognised that observation takes every bit as much planning as direct teaching (Figure 3).

Baseline Assessment

From September 1998 it is a statutory requirement for all maintained primary schools in England to use an accredited baseline assessment scheme with all children starting school, whether in reception classes or Year 1. For the first time in this country it will be mandatory to assess children *before* they begin the formal process of learning. One purpose of baseline assessment is to establish what children already know and can do and thus 'provide information to help teachers plan effectively to meet children's individual learning needs' (SCAA, 1996). But assessment on entry has other functions and in a climate of increasing accountability there is a drive towards establishing what children already know and can do so as to determine the contribution to their learning made by the setting they attend. The second purpose of baseline assessment, then, is to 'measure children's attainment, using one or more numerical outcomes which can be used in later value-added analyses of children's progress' (SCAA, 1996). When considering how effectively this national initiative might meet its two stated purposes it is important to realise that they rely on two quite different forms of assessment.

Purpose 1: planning to meet children's individual learning needs

To plan effectively for children's individual learning needs, as complete a picture as possible must be established of the existing attitudes, knowledge,

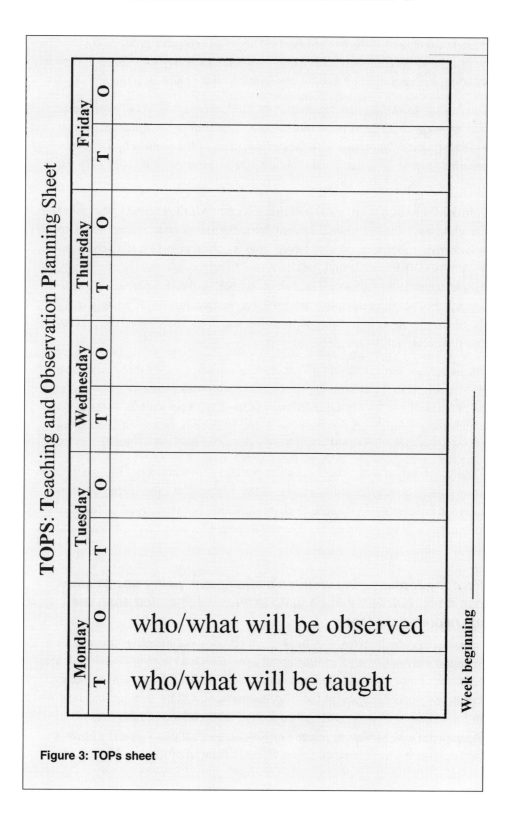

Figure 3: TOPs sheet

understanding and skills of the learner. This is a **formative** process. It starts before the child comes to school and continues each day as a fuller understanding emerges through careful observation of the child in action.

To plan for learning needs, assessments need to be made about everything that we want children to learn more about. This cannot be selective – it is a **holistic** process concerned with the development of the whole child. It is not possible to plan to meet all the child's learning needs with only half the assessment information to hand.

Formative assessment is a **partnership** process. All those who know about the child as a learner should be involved. Formative assessment needs to acknowledge the parents' and carers' role as children's first and enduring educators (DfEE, 1997) and seek to *learn from* parents rather than simply *inform* them. When nurseries and schools seek to build a partnership with parents they should remember that they are, in fact, privileged to be joining the already successful learning partnership which exists between the parents and their children (Fisher, 1996).

Formative assessment should also include what is known by those who have been involved in the children's pre-school education. The nursery, playgroup or pre-school previously attended will often have kept careful records on which the reception teacher can build and will be a source of substantial information about how each child learns and what they know and can do.

Finally, formative assessment involves partnership with the child. No one knows more about the individuality of the learner than the learners themselves. Conversations that seek to elicit children's perceptions of themselves as learners will be a source of influential information about current needs and future plans.

Purpose 2: measuring children's attainment, using one or more numerical outcomes to be used in later value-added analyses of children's progress

Assessment which gives measurable scores is a **summative** process. A judgement is made at a given time about a pre-selected range of issues, which have been numerically graded in terms of achievement. Value-added judgements rely on knowing what the entry assessment will be measured against. In England and Wales it will, in this instance, be children's achievements in the national assessments at the end of Key Stage 1 (at age 7 years). If this is the comparative measure then this is clearly a **limited** process and is not concerned with the full extent of what a child might know or be able to do (physical and creative development are not part of the SCAA baseline assessment 'scales'). Finally, the summative judgement is undertaken by the reception teacher and so there is no requirement – and frequently no opportunity – to draw on the knowledge of other adults involved in the education of the child. The summative judgement is undertaken by the teacher, without consultation, and is therefore likely to be a **solitary** process.

All effective assessments on entry to school include both formative and summative processes. They acknowledge that effective summative judgements cannot be made without drawing on effective formative records. They emphasise the need to have secure evidence of children's learning drawn from a range of experiences, activities, conversations and observations. They recognise that without formative assessment, summative judgements are made on very limited and shaky grounds.

If on-entry assessment is to be of value – which it certainly is – we must recognise its two different functions and employ two different processes. But, more importantly, if both purposes are held to be equally important the two processes must be given equal value. Any worthwhile baseline assessment scheme should confirm that accurate summative assessment can only be achieved by drawing on high quality formative observation and records.

■ Planning

Once a setting has established what a child already knows and can do, practitioners can fine-tune their planning to meet the needs and interests of the individual learners for whom they are responsible. Some planning will have been done before these assessments are made: certain aspects of the learning environment and the curriculum are generally appropriate for most children of a certain age and stage of development. It is the 'customised' planning for the particular children in the setting at that time which is influenced by the assessments of their abilities on entry and after. It is perhaps helpful when thinking about this complex cycle of assessment and planning to think of longer term planning – done weeks or months before the planning is put into practice – as planning the **curriculum**. In other word, this is the 'menu' of skills, understandings, knowledge and attitudes which will be appropriate for most children in this setting for a specified time. Short term planning – done the day or the moment before the planning is put into practice – is planning for the **child.** This is when the 'diet' is selected, modified and customised in order to meet the particular characteristics of individual children.

Educators, then, should be clear about the purposes of the different stages of planning and understand how they are influenced by assessment.

Long term planning is concerned with children's entitlement to a **broad** and **balanced** curriculum and is achieved through the appropriate allocation of time to the teaching and assessment of the Desirable Outcomes for Children's Learning (SCAA, 1996), the National Curriculum, religious education and other curriculum aspects identified by the setting.

Medium term planning addresses **continuity** and **progression** from one stage in each area of learning to the next, and from one setting or class to the next, drawing on schemes of work, curriculum policies and the long term plan and identifying the concepts, skills, knowledge and attitudes to which children will be introduced over a specified time. It is at this stage that the curriculum may be seen to be most effectively organised by linking together different areas of learning through themes or topics.

Short term planning is concerned with **differentiation** and planning for the needs of specific groups and individual children. It provides the detail of activities, experiences, resources, groupings and teaching strategies which are identified through ongoing observation and assessment of children in action.

The whole planning process must be embedded in the aims and objectives of the individual setting. A setting's aims should be the result of careful examination by staff, parents, children and the governing or managing committees responsible. Aims should reflect the individual purposes and direction of the setting and encompass all elements of its work including children's learning, ethos, parental involvement and links with the community. Only when a setting is clear about its aims and purposes can what is to be planned and how be resolved. There are so many decisions to be made about the development of a setting that without clear aims it is difficult to prioritise what should happen and in which order.

Long Term Plans

Long term plans should cover the length of time that children spend in a setting. In schools this can mean a plan covering ages 3 to 11 years. In a playgroup or nursery school it may mean three or five terms, but whatever the period, planning should demonstrate that educators have thought through the entire learning experience for the children. Consideration needs to be given to whether the planned programme covers all essential elements of the given curriculum and how other aspects of importance to the setting are to be included. In the education of children under 6 years, all areas of learning are likely to be included in their daily experiences. However, it may be that certain aspects *within* those areas of learning are emphasised in different ways from one term or space of time to the next. In mathematics, for example, size

The Stages of Planning

long term planning

evidence of
- breadth and balance
- curriculum coverage
- hourages

drawing on

- desirable outcomes
- national curriculum programmes of study

medium term planning

evidence of
- progression and continuity
- termly concepts, skills, knowledge, attitudes to be taught
- integrated and subject specific work

drawing on

- long term plan
- curriculum policies
- schemes of work

short term planning (weekly)

evidence of
- differentiation
- intended learning
- activities
- support
- resourcing
- assessment
- evaluation

drawing on

- medium term plans
- observations of children
- assessment of previous learning
- evaluation of previous lessons

c:jf/nh7

Figure 4: The stages of planning

might be emphasised through the creation of a shoe shop in the imaginative area in the Spring term, and weighing emphasised in the baby clinic in the Summer term. The following chart captures how different parts of each area of learning are emphasised in different terms, according to the number of terms children spend in the setting.

How does assessment inform long term planning?

Assessment of children's learning and progress can inform long term planning by revealing whether children have experienced a broad and balanced curriculum and whether children have been assessed across the full range of their experiences. Assessment can show whether children have received their entitlement to all elements of the Desirable Outcomes (SCAA, 1996) and the National Curriculum, and can support practitioners in reviewing the total sum of children's experiences during their time in the setting.

Medium term plans

Medium term planning is crucial in establishing what is to be taught over a specified period. For younger children that may be half a term, three weeks or a few days. The medium term plan should show both what is to be learnt as part of the theme or topic i.e. investigating heavier/lighter than; prints using *The Enormous Turnip*, and what will be happening on an ongoing basis alongside the topic based activities i.e. establishing an understanding of print from left to right, number rhymes for addition and subtraction, development of fine motor skills through handling scissors and staplers. Figure 6 shows a medium term plan which records the intended learning for a given period of time. Figure 7 shows how the intended learning that is to be integrated into a topic (recorded in the shaded area) is happening alongside learning which does not fit into the topic (the white area).

The most effective medium term plans draw on schemes of work that show the progression of concepts, skills, knowledge and attitudes in each area of learning. Once children have begun to differentiate between the number of surfaces and corners on a triangle or rectangle what concept or understanding should be planned for next? There are two helpful documents from Oxford-shire practitioners (Roberts, 1995; van Santen and Auty, 1997) which give practical support for planning an appropriate curriculum both at this stage and at the stage of short term planning.

Topic work

Areas of learning can be linked together into themes or topics if appropriate at the medium term stage (Figure 7). There has been an increase lately in the

long-term planning (breadth and balance)
the emphasis in each term

	term 1	term 2	term 3
personal & social development			
language & literacy			
mathematics			
knowledge & understanding of the world			
physical development			
creative development			

Figure 5: Long-term planning sheet.

MEDIUM TERM PLANNING
(continuity and progression)

Area of Learning

Desirable Outcome	Intended Learning	Possible Activities	Targets for achievement	Evaluations
	• concepts/ understanding • skills • knowledge • attitudes	• can be selected now but preferably when children's needs and interests are better known	• by the end of unit of work • differentiated into broad levels	• what covered • what missed • what change

Figure 6: Medium Term Plan (continuity and progression)

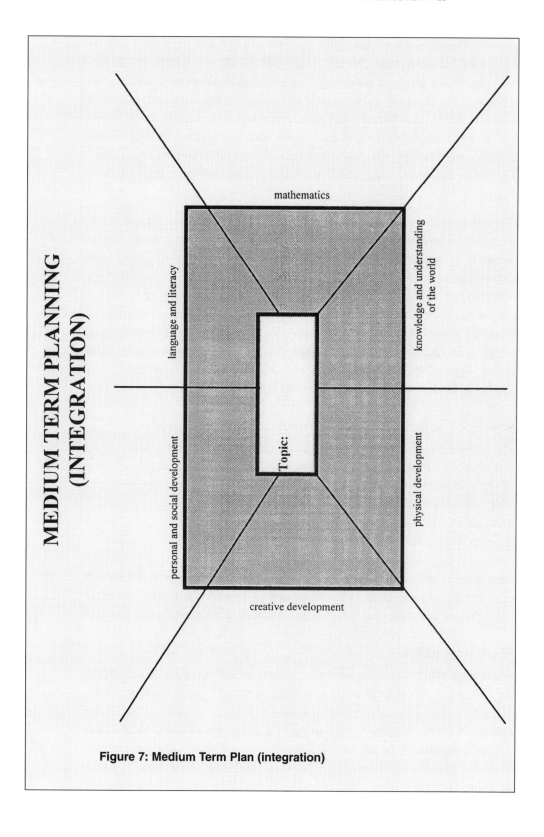

Figure 7: Medium Term Plan (integration)

extent of topics and how long they last. Remember that topics are usually more useful to adults than children; it is generally adults who like the framework that topics give in drawing together activities and experiences under the umbrella of a title such as 'ourselves' or 'homes'. Children's understanding naturally draws on different areas of learning and makes links that are relevant and meaningful to them as individuals. But all too often the links made in topics are made by adults and can be baffling and irrelevant to children. The links made must make children's learning more coherent and not more confusing.

It is valuable not only to be clear about progression within each area of learning but to establish the potential learning in each area of the setting. Play is central to the learning of young children and all appropriate settings will have a wide range of opportunities for children to engage in play, including 'freeflow' play (Bruce, 1991) throughout the day. Educators usually know which areas are considered valuable in their potential for learning but cannot always articulate this to parents and managers. Some excellent staff development work can be done by discussing the potential for learning in each area of the setting. Figure 6 shows a planning sheet by the Oxfordshire Early Years Team which has unpicked the potential learning in the area of malleable materials.

How does assessment inform medium term planning?

The assessment of children's learning can inform medium term planning in two ways. Firstly, assessment can show whether the planned experiences for children on entry to a setting are significantly different from those of a child ready to transfer to school. It reveals whether there is sufficient progression in children's learning (as individuals and as a group) and whether the planned learning was successful in giving continuity of experience. Secondly, assessment can show whether planning has been coherent in bringing together strands from different areas of learning into themes or topics. Children's involvement and response to activities and experiences will show whether these themes and topics are relevant and meaningful to them as learners.

Short term plans

While long term plans and medium term plans are concerned with organising the curriculum, short term plans are concerned with planning for the child. The curriculum becomes differentiated to meet the specific needs of the group of children that are in the setting in a given year or term. Most of the detail should already be in place. *What* is to be taught has already been established at the long and medium term stage and now is the time to make decisions about *how* these concepts, skills, knowledge and attitudes are to be

Language & Literacy

Concepts and Knowledge:
- that we can create imaginary worlds
- that we can use descriptive and comparative language

Skills:
- communicating ideas
- imaging to create a scene
- creating imaginary worlds
- learning new vocabulary
- negotiating

Attitudes:
- the wish to communicate
- the ability to empathise and tryout different roles vicariously

Mathematical

Concepts and Knowledge:
- that there is 1 to 1 correspondence
- that there are different shapes which have names
- that comparisons can be made in respect of weight, shape and size, colour
- that shape can change but weight does not

Skills:
- counting
- patterning
- weighing
- measuring
- estimating
- matching
- sorting
- ordering

Attitudes:
- skills can be improved
- the wonder of pattern
- the wonder of infinity

Aesthetic & Creative

Concepts and Knowledge:
- that different sculptures, pots, forms, plates jugs can be created
- that these can be useful, beautiful and inspirational
- that the surface texture can be changed
- the material can be changed

Skills:
- making models, pots, forms, pushing, moulding, rolling, pulling, making patterns, cutting, bending, imprinting, smoothing, squeezing, creating something, stroking, pinching

Attitudes:
- enjoying tactile experience
- wonder at the creativity of human race
- you have the power to make what you like

Physical

Concepts and Knowledge:
- understanding the capabilities of hands

Skills:
- using tools
- manual dexterity - fine motor (gross motor if working with large amounts of clay)
- manual strength - fine motor

Attitudes:
- the confidence that comes with successful exploration and practise
- motor skills are empowering

Knowledge and Understanding of the World

Personal, Spiritual & Moral

Concepts and Knowledge:
- that we can make/play with others or alone

Skills:
- sharing, turn taking
- copying
- role modelling
- respecting the needs of other
- creating something

Attitudes:
- that creating something is satisfying
- that empathy/valuing anothers work can be a connecting experience

Human & Social

Concepts and Knowledge:
- that forms pots and sculptures can be different if they came from different parts of the world
- that forms pots and sculptures were made and used in the past

Skills:
- enquiry
- observing similarities and differences

Attitudes:
- awareness of the skills of other people in different countries and in the past

Science

Concepts and Knowledge:
- materials and how they can change eg. using ingredients to make dough; water with clay and then leaving to dry; manipulating different shapes; when warm and cold different materials behave in different ways

Skills:
- experimenting
- hypothesising

Attitudes:
- investigation
- curiosity in the material

Design & Technology

Concepts and Knowledge:
- of tools and understanding their use
- that a technique can be learnt and repeated

Skills:
- making plans
- use of tools - cutting, slicing, spreading
- planning

Attitudes:
- confidence to use different tools

Figure 8: The potential learning in malleable materials

introduced to the children in ways that are relevant and meaningful. Short term planning should address:

• *Previous experience*

It is crucial that children's current curriculum is embedded in their previous learning. Children make connections most successfully when links between their past and present learning are made explicit. Children understand most readily when they can fit their new knowledge into the understandings they already have. Short term planning – particularly plans for adult-focused activities or small group times – should show what is significant and relevant in children's previous experience to the activity about to be undertaken.

• *Intended learning*

This is taken straight from the medium term plans. It is useful to re-establish, for all adults, what it is intended that children should learn in the course of an activity or experience.

• *Selected activity*

Activities should be chosen to bring about intended learning. Some activities will be more prescriptive than others. There are usually three main types of activity in a good learning environment: adult focused, adult initiated and child initiated.

Adult focused activities are those at which the adult intends to stay and work alongside a child or children. They usually have precise learning intentions and adults stay with an individual or group to realise them. These activities are usually the most directed and outcomes are fairly predictable.

Adult initiated activities are activities which adults initiate and then leave. When adults select the activity and the resources they have clear learning intentions in mind but because they will not stay with the activity they know that children's own interests or concerns may cause the activity's outcome to change course. These activities need to be relatively open ended and exploratory so that children are not dependent on adults for support and progress until the adult is ready to come to them.

Child initiated activities are activities where the outcome is not predictable. Adults will have considered the potential for learning in certain areas and resources within the setting (see Figure 8). However when children initiate their own learning they are free to take resources and ideas and explore and extend them in their own creative ways. Such experience – which most often occurs in play – 'motivates and challenges the participant both to master what is familiar and to respond to the unfamiliar in terms of gaining information, knowledge, skills and understandings' (Moyles, 1989 p7).

• Location

Decide where learning will most effectively take place. The outdoor area for learning is a critical feature of the best early years provision and adults need to make decisions about whether a planned activity is best located indoors or out.

• Resources

There are many resources which practitioners have to gather together in advance if activities are to go smoothly. A whole range of resources is available daily in early years settings. But others, such as a visit or visitor, or photographs and artefacts may be needed at special times for certain occasions, and planning needs to ensure that these are organised and prepared in time.

• Groupings

Young children collaborate naturally when they see the need to do so. But sometimes an adult wants certain children to work together for a particular reason which may be concerned with gender, age, ethnicity or stage of development. Either way planning is important. If children are to see a purpose in working together then activities and resources must encourage collaboration and co-operation. If adults want children to learn in a specific social context then this needs to be defined in planning.

• Adult support

The role of adults in children's learning should be clearly defined in planning. For each kind of activity outlined earlier, the educator's role is crucial but different.

Adult focused activities: the role of the educator is concerned primarily with teaching. In other words, by being alongside the learner(s) the adult is able to demonstrate, explain, question and challenge in ways that support the achievement of the intended learning.

Adult initiated activities: the role of the adult is particularly important in the planning and assessment stages. The adult must select an activity which is likely to bring about the intended learning, when children are independently engaged on it. The adult has far less direct influence that in an adult focused task but must rely on their professional skill in choosing an activity to encourage children to achieve autonomously. This does not mean that children are abandoned. Independent learners should not be abandoned learners. When the adult has finished her adult focused activity she must go to all other groups and individuals to assess their progress in their various tasks. Then is the time for the adult to question, ask for explanations, make suggestions and to assess what children have been learning and judge whether the selected activity brought about the learning intended.

Child initiated activities: the role of the adult here focuses on the stages of intervention and assessment. The adult plans the areas and resources and thus has some influence on the learning which follows. But generally adults will not know what direction the learning will take until they observe and perhaps join in with the activity at an appropriate stage. High quality play needs skilled adult intervention – intervention and not interference. It is all too easy to make hasty judgements about children's play and to intervene in ways which are inappropriate and which might well bring it to a premature halt. In assessing the skills and understandings that children are displaying in their self-chosen activities, educators are also evaluating their own provision and support for that learning.

• *Evidence of learning*

Before an activity begins, it is helpful to establish what will give educators evidence of children's learning. With young children much of this evidence is in the processes of learning rather than the outcomes. Deciding whether it is children's talk or their actions which will provide the evidence from which assessments will be made ensures that an adult is in the right place at the right time, looking and listening for the right things.

• *Evaluation*

Evaluation is concerned with the effectiveness of the educator. Was the right activity selected to bring about the intended learning? Evaluation challenges practitioners to reflect on their preparation, teaching skills and curriculum planning. It is here that notes can be made to adjust or refine future planning.

Differentiation

Short term planning meets the needs of specific learners because it differentiates the curriculum for different needs. Differentiation is achieved in two ways, firstly by **outcome** and secondly by **input**:

differentiation by outcome	one activity meets the learning needs of a wide range of abilities because of its open ended nature

differentiation by input	specific activities/experiences/outcomes are planned to meet the specific learning needs of a particular individual or group at a particular time.

what can be differentiated?

tasks/activities/experiences

- will the intended learning be best achieved by varying the activity according to different children's particular interests?

introductions/summing up/rounding off

- do different children or groups of children need the activity introduced or concluded in different ways?

- do some need more detailed explanations whilst others need practical demonstration?

processes

- do all children need to go through the same process to arrive at a desirable outcome?

- how can the process be made sufficiently flexible to meet all learning styles and strategies?

outcomes

- are the outcomes of learning sufficiently open to allow all children to achieve?

- can all children demonstrate what they know and can do?

- will the outcome give each learner a feeling of personal satisfaction and achievement?

support

- do learners need a high level of support at this moment or will they do better to work independently?

- what is the nature of the support they need? (do they need direct instruction, questioning or observing?)

- if children are working independently do they know how to find resources and where to go for help?

groupings

- are children best working alone or in a group?

- do they need to be put with certain children or to choose their peers to work with?

- if they are being required to work as a group is the task a collaborative one?

resources

• does every child need the same resources to achieve the same ends?

• do some children's special needs mean the acquisition of specialised resources to meet their needs?

Short term planning is about differentiation. This does not mean that every child has an individualised programme all the time. Children have many similarities as well as differences in their learning needs. What is important is to know what children need, rather than guess or presume.

How does assessment inform short term planning?

When early childhood educators observe and converse with children they are gathering evidence of their learning. Specialist practitioners can then analyse what they see and hear and make judgements about what individual children know, understand and can do. These observations and conversations are the substance of daily/weekly professional dialogue between practitioners working in the same setting. By sharing what they have heard and seen, practitioners can refine their short term plans to meet the current needs of children.

■ Assessment that follows planning and teaching

Assessment that follows planning and teaching evaluates not only children's learning but also the quality of teaching. This is the stage in the cycle when educators ask: what have children learnt and how successful was my planning and teaching in bringing this about?

Assessment which results in action

As we have seen, there is no point in undertaking any kind of assessment unless something is done with the results. Assessment has a function only if the results inform something or someone. Before deciding which form of assessment to use we must be clear about the purposes of that assessment. Gipps (1994) suggests that there are two assessment functions: to provide information *outside* the classroom and to provide information within the classroom. She is clear that it is not efficacious to use one assessment across a range of purposes. The criterion for selection must be 'fitness for purpose' and educators should know their purpose before choosing their assessment tool.

If assessment is to instruct the educator it needs to be *formative*. It is a daily, on-going part of the teaching and learning cycle whereby the educator observes what children know and understand and can do in so as to plan what they need to know and do next.

ADULT FOCUSED ACTIVITY

Name of Adult ....

Area of curriculum
Previous knowledge
What do I want the children to learn
Activity
Differentiation
Targeted children
Resources
Time
Evaluation
Forward planning

Figure 9: Adult focused activity planning sheet

Formative assessment has the following features:

- it is an integral part of teaching and learning

- it is ongoing, cumulative records, taken throughout the teaching day

- it accepts contributions from parents, children and other adults who work with the child

- it provides evidence on which to base future planning

- it incorporates analysis and planned action.

Assessment to inform others ('outside' the classroom) requires a summative procedure. The 'outsider' does not need – and is unlikely to read – a considerable amount of accumulated formative information but rather a summary of where the child is now in terms of attainment and development. Summative judgements are made in two ways. Firstly, as part of practitioner assessment – a summary made to pass on to the next educator or parent or other professional. Secondly, as an external test where nothing is drawn from previous knowledge or expectations but a judgement is made using an instrument, such as a test, administered in order to assess a child's ability in a prescribed and usually quite limited range of things.

Summative assessment has the following features:

- it provides brief statements made to summarise information about achievements

- it is gleaned from formative information

- it takes the form of check/tick lists

- it summmarises the most vital and relevant information about what the child knows, understands and can do

- it is made at a point of transfer e.g. entry; change of setting; new class/school

- it is designed to inform others e.g. parents; next teacher/school; outside agencies.

Assessing the quality of learning

Educators should assess the quality of children's learning both *during* and *after* an activity or experience. During the activity educators can gather first hand evidence of what children say and what they do, which will reveal what they already know and what they are learning. So adults need to make observations of children in action and ask:

- what are the child's attitudes to learning?

- what are the child's strategies for learning?

- what skills is the child demonstrating?

- what understandings – and misunderstandings – is the child revealing?

Observations must be both *systematic* and *spontaneous.* A simple card index carrying every child's name can be rotated so that each in turn becomes 'child of the day'. These assessments are most useful when targeted, the adults identifying precisely what they are going to look for and listen for and why, before each activity. However, learning occurs when it has not been planned! So it is equally important to ensure that when children demonstrate their ability to do or understand something which was not part of the setting's planned curriculum, there are procedures for capturing and recording these achievements also.

Adults cannot be alongside every child all the time, so some assessments have to be done when an activity is over. Skilled questioning and dialogue with children should allow children to describe and explain what they have done and learnt. The adult needs to establish:

- what did the child enjoy?

- what did the child experience?

- what did the child achieve?

- what were their chosen strategies?

- did the child understand the task (if it was adult directed)?

- did the child come to the intended learning (if it was adult initiated)?

- if not, why not?

- what does the child want to know or experience next?

Recording

Educators are making assessments about learning throughout the day. It is impossible to remember all the significant moments of learning and so adults need ways of recording learning which are *valuable* and *manageable*. There are five aspects of assessment which all educators need to implement:

jottings: daily notes which remind the educator of what children have said and or done and which gives evidence of learning and development or concern;

staff review: a regular time when all those concerned with the education of a certain group of children get together to discuss individuals and share knowledge and information;

formative records: record sheets which are designed to capture the significant moments in children's learning and/or development. They arise from daily jottings and/or regular review by staff.

summative records: drawn from on-going formative records, these are made at a certain time for a certain purpose which might be: transfer to another setting; reporting to parents;or reporting to outside agencies e.g. an educational psychologist.

individual profiles of work: both formative and summative processes are substantiated by the maintenance of individual profiles of children's work – a collection of pieces of their work across all areas of learning, showing evidence of progression in skills and understanding. The selection should be manageable and it must be decided how many pieces will be saved, how often and who will make the selection. Profiles of work are usually highly valued by parents and children and should be a personal history of children's development during their time in the setting.

Because these profiles are most frequently used retrospectively there should be sufficient information for anyone who sees them – parents, other educators, inspectors and children – to be given a context in which to make analyses about the validity of the evidence collected and the progress made. Annotation of work in children's profiles should include the child's name, the date, the context, the level of support from other children/adults (if any), the child's commentary (if any) and the Desirable Outcome/National Curriculum level (if appropriate).

Recall time

Another highly effective way of assessing children after they have completed an activity is to talk with them during a planned recall or review time. At recall time children explain and describe to other children what they have done and/or learnt in the course of an activity. Recall time shows children that their independent work (whether adult initiated or self-initiated) will be shared and received. It gives educators the opportunity to listen and make assessments of children as they talk. Recall time must be built into the teaching day and can and should happen at different times of the day. Because of the concentration span of children – and adults – it is recommended that no more than five or six children recall at any one session (depending on children's age and stage of development). It is important to remember that recall is a time when **children** do the talking, not adults.

For *children*, recall time offers opportunities to:

- use language and communicate for a purpose
- engage in speaking and listening in a small or larger group
- think things through out loud
- describe what they have done in both child initiated and adult initiated activities
- explain how they went about things and what resources and/or materials they used
- share what they enjoyed or found hard
- consider what they would like to try next.

For *adults*, recall time is an opportunity to:

- hear how the child went about things and the strategies they used
- listen to a child's developing understandings and misunderstandings about things
- record what the child says as evidence of learning
- think about their planning in relation to what the child seems to have experienced.

Self-assessment

Recall time is one way in which educators encourage children to reflect on their own experiences and share evaluating them. Some teachers also work with children to identify 'success criteria' (or targets for achievement) before a task begins, so that children are clear about the purpose of the task and can judge for themselves what they have achieved. This leads to intrinsic motivation because there is greater ownership of the task and children are less reliant on the adults for approval and reward. Experiences are made far more purposeful for children when they are involved in the evaluation of their learning in this way.

Educators should also be engaged in self-assessment. Reflection on the actions of assessment, planning and teaching enables practitioners to identify their personal and professional areas for development. It requires them to be flexible in their approaches to teaching and learning and to be willing to analyse their current practice rigorously to bring about change that will benefit the children as learners. At the end of a session it is important to reflect on these questions:

- did the child/children learn what I intended they should learn?
- if not, why not?
- if not, did they learn something else?
- what does this teach me about the child/children?
- what would I change if I had to do the activity again?
- do I need to change/adjust my short term plans as a result of today's experiences?

How educators go about this evaluation will vary. For some it will be part of the daily evaluation of the session within the setting when staff meet together to review the day and its outcomes. For some there will be a requirement to write a brief evaluation on their planning sheets. Both strategies are effective in encouraging the process of reflection and a good way of demonstrating that assessment informs future planning.

■ Conclusion

At the beginning of this chapter I asked which comes first, planning or assessment? This chapter has sought to demonstrate that in reality they function in a continuous cycle, with assessment informing planning which informs assessment which influences planning. One thing is certain, planning cannot be effective unless assessment is effective. Educators in all early years settings must continue to develop and refine their planning and assessment practices if they are to be truly effective in supporting young children as learners.

References

Blenkin G.M. and Kelly A.V. (Eds) (1987) *Early Childhood Education: a developmental curriculum* London: Paul Chapman

Bruce, T. (1987) *Early Childhood Education* Sevenoaks: Hodder and Stoughton

Bruce, T. (1991) *Time to Play in Early Childhood Education* Sevenoaks: Hodder and Stoughton

DfEE, (1997) *Excellence in Schools* London: HMSO.

Fisher, J. (1996) *Starting from the Child?* Buckingham: Open University Press

Gardner, H. (1993) *The Unschooled Mind* London: Fontana Press

Gipps, C.V. (1994) *Beyond Testing* London: The Falmer Press

Hurst, V. and Lally, M.(1992) 'Assessment in Nursery Education: A Review of Approaches' in G.M. Blenkin and A.V. Kelly (Eds) *Assessment in Early Childhood Education* London: Paul Chapman

Hutchin, V. (1996) *Tracking Significant Achievement in the Early Years* London: Hodder and Stoughton

Moyles, J.R. (1989) *Just Playing?* Milton Keynes: Open University Press

National Commission on Education, (1993) *Learning to Succeed* London: Heinemann

Pollard, A. (1996) *The Social World of Children's Learning* London: Cassell

Roberts, R. (Ed) (1995) *A Nursery Education Curriculum for the Early Years* Oxford: National Primary Centre

SCAA, (1996) *Desirable Outcomes for Children's Learning on Entering Compulsory Education* London: DfEE

SCAA, (1997) *The National Framework for Baseline Assessment* SCAA, London

van Santen, L. and Auty, M. (1997) *Nursery Planning for Learning Outcomes* Oxford: National Primary Centre

Wood, D., Bruner, J.S. and Ross, G. (1976) The role of tutoring in problem solving *Journal of Child Psychology and Psychiatry* 17(2): 89-100

PART II

CORE LEARNING EXPERIENCES

CHAPTER 3

CURIOSITY AND COMMUNICATION: LANGUAGE AND LITERACY IN THE EARLY YEARS

Jeni Riley

It is testament to Margaret Donaldson's observation that 'children are highly active and efficient learners, competent enquirers, eager to understand' (1989, p36) that the majority of young children demonstrate impressive oral competence in at least one language. This chapter re-affirms the centrality of language and literacy in the early years curriculum. It shows how both spoken and written language are learned through young children's curiosity and desire to make sense of the world; that each mode of language powerfully supports the development of the other, in a close inter-relationship; and that through increasing control of oracy and then literacy children acquire ways to access knowledge and also the tools with which to think and learn.

Adults in the nursery or playgroup will be aware of their role in supporting the development of their pupils' oral abilities and enabling them to become effective communicators in a variety of situations and for many purposes. They are best placed to do this if they acknowledge the importance of speaking and listening and understand clearly the links that can be made with reading and writing. The young child gradually becomes aware of the relationship between spoken and written language through many varied and meaningful encounters with print.

Developing Oracy

The SCAA (1996) Desirable Outcomes document states :

> In small and large groups, children listen attentively and talk about their experiences. They use a growing vocabulary with increasing fluency to express thoughts and convey meaning to the listener.

The Learning Environment

Language, whether spoken or written, cannot flourish in a vacuum. Children will seize on opportunities to communicate, question, solve problems, wonder, debate, argue and listen in an environment that is supportive, stimulating and challenging in its provision of rich experiences and activities. The most valuable learning opportunities for children to use language are purposeful situations; those that build on previous learning and are embedded in their reality.

The establishment of an environment which motivates children to speak and interact will include quiet and busy areas, interest tables and displays, topic or special focus-related resources, construction materials and manipulation activities, in addition to an inviting supply of educational toys. Activities of this type and also the experiences that provide an opportunity for pre-schoolers to talk through new concepts, to relive past events, to hypothesise and to experiment with new ideas which give rise to the use of written language, naturally and meaningfully, are all essential for language development. For example, a discussion in anticipation of a visit from a member of the local fire brigade will involve arrangements to bake biscuits in welcome and to organise the classroom so everyone can see and touch equipment. Stories and reference books will be read on the topic and thank you cards will be designed, made, written and sent after the visit. Every occasion can be utilised to maximum advantage.

In addition, the learning environment that generates the rich use of language will provide for the children to engage in make-believe and role-play.

Imaginative play

> Purposeful play features strongly in good pre-school education. It is not a free or wholly unstructured activity. Through the selection of materials and equipment... teachers ensure that, in their play children encounter the learning experiences intended... Play that is well planned and pleasurable helps children to think, to increase their understanding and to improve their language competence. It allows children to be creative, to explore and investigate materials, to experiment and to draw and test their conclusions. (DES, 1989, p8)

The home corner exists in all nurseries and most playgroups but sometimes it is in need of revitalising. Role-play can be transformed by the addition of a tyre, a steering wheel, a rope, large building blocks, giant cardboard boxes and telephones. Supplying a dressing-up box with new hats, shoes, bags, jewellery such as strings of beads, belts, veils, sunglasses, masks and cloaks will stimulate curiosity in a previously well but traditionally used home area. Environmental print e.g. message boards and pads, telephone books and calendars will make literacy an integral part of the role-play; similarly, supplying writing materials will encourage the production of shopping lists, letters, and the making and sending of greetings cards.

Areas for role-play that have been designed on a theme, often after a local visit, are powerful vehicles for developing spoken and written language. The transformation of an area of the nursery into a Post Office, a McDonalds' or a cafe, a doctor's surgery, a baby clinic or a hospital, an optician, a fish and chip shop, an Indian or Chinese take-away restaurant, a hairdressing salon [minus sharp scissors!], all offer many opportunities to discuss, plan and learn technical or specialist vocabulary, to equip through making and finding, to write and to read with adult support.

Even the traditional mini-supermarket or shop with the predictable range of boxes, food packets and cartons brought from home can be transformed [after discussion and a majority vote] into a chemist, newsagent or baker's shop the latter involving much modelling and the later painting of flour and water dough cakes, biscuits, samosas, chapatis, spring rolls and buns. Items such as shopping bags [hand-printed with the nursery shop logo and name!], a cash register, money, purses, trolleys, scales, the week's best buy 'special offer' posters and notepads for shopping lists all enhance the role-play and provide a genuine opportunity to use language for and with real purpose.

Thus the child provided with the appropriate experiences will use speaking and listening in the following dimensions in order to: act on and give instructions; respond to and make suggestions; ask and answer questions; challenge ideas; hold conversations; describe and discuss; offer explanations and evaluations; negotiate; persuade; reason; share experience, opinion and emotion; speculate and hypothesise; think, re-think and shape ideas and plans; and express themselves with increasing clarity. The child is learning '...to turn language and thought in upon [her/himself]...not just to talk, but to choose what he will say, not to interpret but to weigh possible interpretations. His conceptual system must expand in the direction of increasing ability to represent itself' (Donaldson, 1978, p88-89).

Bilingual Learners

The principles and examples of good practice suggested so far will inform the basis of working with all 3-6 year-olds. However, there may be a need for specific support for children for whom English is as an additional language (EAL), and who are at various stages of developing their linguistic competence within the early years setting. These children may be bilingual, tri-lingual or multilingual and will bring a wide variety of experience, usage and proficiency in their first and additional languages. Some settings may have substantial numbers of bilingual learners with one dominant first language, others may have small groups or individual learners speaking a range of home languages. The children attending early years settings in Britain represent several different categories of bilingual learner, at various stages of competence in English, some may have arrived recently in Britain for a range of reasons; others (95%) are British born.

Whilst the National Curriculum is explicit about the responsibility of all educational institutions to enable every pupil to communicate successfully in English – and this includes awareness of and the appropriate use of Standard English – there is research evidence that identifies the most favourable conditions for learning of a second language effectively. If, firstly, it is developed from the basis of a flourishing, maintained and supported first language (Cummins, 1979) and if, secondly, this language is also respected and encouraged (ILEA,1990) progress in the additional language is enhanced. Developing the child's spoken and written English provides him/her with access to the whole curriculum, to social interaction and to personal opportunity and power. The attitudes of the adults with whom the child comes in contact are crucial in promoting these principles, particularly as early years educators are seen by both children and their parents as representatives of the whole educational system. A positive attitude will be demonstrated through both the general policies and good classroom practice and this chapter focuses on the latter.

The principle governing the education of bilingual children is underpinned with the ideology of all early years education encapsulated in the maxim 'observe, support and extend learning'. Adults will first establish what each child can do and understand through observation and assessment, the planning required for the next stage of learning using the motivating force of the child's interests and strengths as a starting point, as suggested in Chapter 2. The most effective way of working in a setting with bilingual pupils is to integrate the appropriate language support fully into practice which has a meaningful, active context. Acquiring or developing an additional language demands high levels of risk on the part of the learner. So the ethos of the classroom must allow the children to feel secure in the knowledge that their home or community language is valued and respected. This is achieved through the positive promotion of the first language, encouraging the pupils to use it, perhaps inviting other children or parents to act as interpreters for key events and for activities needing specific explanation, or translating favourite and class-made books into an additional language. Songs, rhymes and stories can be enjoyed in the children's first languages.

Children who are in the very early stages of learning English as a second or additional language are aware of the communicative purpose and function of a language but will go through similar stages of English acquisition to the young infant, but accelerated. Initially there is a period of silence, when the child has an increasing receptive language capability indicated by what he/she can understand but appears to have little or no productive ability. Communication will occur through gesture, mood and non-verbal utterance. The next stage generates single words such as 'yes', 'me', 'no', 'OK', 'see' etc. Children then gradually begin to put together two or three words to express themselves in increasingly more complex ways, for example 'Me too' and 'Me go too?', 'Come see', 'Go away!' with gesture and intonation appropriately emphasising their intention. It may take up to two years for children to achieve fluency in face-to-face contextually supportive situations and much longer to use oral language accurately in abstract situations (Cummins, 1984a).

During additional language acquisition the adults with whom the bilingual pupils are in daily contact have considerable opportunity to facilitate their progress. That they understand what is being said is crucial and they are helped by visual and contextual support. Instructions or explanations are best accompanied by practical demonstration, lively gestures, intonation, eye contact and frequent repetition. Sensitively grouping children at different stages of competence will help to provide the appropriate linguistic support in imaginative play and other activities; putting them with English mother-tongue children on most occasions, and on others, with an adult.

Specific suggestions to develop oracy might include speaking and listening activities in a small group (with adult support) such as discussion and feed-back sessions, nursery rhymes, 'reading' a large text, games with repetition, imitation and action such as 'Simon Says...', games involving naming and counting such as pelmanism and animal dominoes, various sorting and matching activities, listening and re-telling stories using a story board, 'fuzzy-felts' or puppets, adult-made books with repetitive structures such as

'Faziah likes drawing but Mahmood likes painting' and the positive inclusion of all the pupils in class routines, taking messages and undertaking 'jobs'. The emphasis at this stage will be on engaging children in practical, activity based learning such as cooking, science and technology where the vocabulary used is embedded in the context of the activity and the understanding is supported by the 'doing'.

Developing Literacy

Quality early years provision will advance the spoken language development of the children and also offer opportunities for valuable literacy learning. Whilst it is generally agreed that being successful in learning to read in the early years of schooling is essential for academic achievement, precisely which of the many approaches and methods most effectively enables children to learn to read and write has still not been universally agreed and remains a matter of contention among educationalists.

This is because the literacy process is a complex one; and this has led to misunderstandings and over-simplification about what is required for children to become fluent readers and writers early in their school careers. However, recent research findings (see Riley, 1996) are clarifying the situation for those who work in early years education.

Marilyn Jaeger Adams (1990) who was commissioned by the American government to review comprehensively recent research into reading, has des-

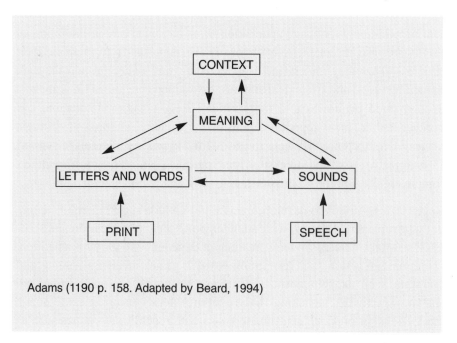

Adams (1190 p. 158. Adapted by Beard, 1994)

cribed the literacy process as having several different aspects that operate together to allow the individual to process text. There is evidence that children who experience teaching that aims to develop **both** the **'top-down' i.e. the meaning-making skills** and the **'bottom-up' i.e. the de-coding skills of print and sound identification** in a **balanced** programme, learn to read and write more successfully and quickly than those who do not; and adults who are aware of the multi-facetedness of the literacy process are more able to provide a variety of appropriate teaching approaches.

The diagram opposite shows clearly the way in which the different aspects of the literacy process inter-relate to enable reading to occur. This is a helpful model for the adult to bear in mind when working with and supporting young children.

The Literacy Process

'Top-down' and 'Bottom-up' processing skills

It can be seen that at the **centre** of the reading act lies **meaning,** which fulfils the whole purpose of the activity. The **context** of the story or sentence allows the reader to support the task of de-coding so as to predict what the words might be in the search for meaning. The use of **context** is described as the **'top-down'** reading skill and this can be encouraged by the adult reading a story to ask children, for example, 'What do you think is going to happen now?' or 'What is he going to say to the Mother Bear?'.

The use of context cues also includes predicting what kind of word might be expected in the text according to the rules of language or **grammar**. In this instance the adult might ask the child encountering an unknown word: 'What do you think will make **sense** here? what **sort** of a word will fit here?'. This way of working with even very young children encourages them to realise the meaning-gaining, active process that reading is.

To learn to read, children have also to be able to hear and distinguish between the different sounds in words and to map them onto letters and groups of letters on the printed page (**phonemic segmentation**). This is increasingly being recognised as a crucial ability and an essential element of reading and writing. Development can be enhanced by practising breaking words into their component sounds, in different and enjoyable ways. This aspect of reading is demonstrated in the diagram; the appreciation of both the visual aspects of print and the aural sounds of spoken language develop side by side, they complement each other and are inter-related. This processing, the **'bottom-up'** or de-**coding skills**, can be developed not only through sharing picture books with children and so implicitly generating meaning from the printed text and drawing on the illustrations but also by directly pointing to words as they are read aloud, occasionally distinguishing between different words and pointing out those that are high frequency (or key words), distinctive or highly patterned, and words that begin with the same letter and sound as the child's name and so familiar and easily identified.

Emergent Literacy

A growing body of research evidence shows the impressive extent of the rich store of knowledge about literacy that children acquire before formal schooling begins. This fascinating work demonstrates the understandings that children develop incidentally and naturally, from the age of about 6 months, from living in a print-filled world. This learning is often shown most clearly through their writing or **mark-making**. The role of the adult in early years settings is to capitalise on this early learning, to be diagnostic of the children in her care, of the stage that each child has reached and to be aware of the nature of the learning that has to occur for children to progress towards conventional literacy.

The first steps on the path to fluent reading

Many educators will know about the work of Marie Clay, which emphasises that the first crucial step on the path towards reading is the pre-requisite understanding of the communicative function of print and, encompassed within that, the realisation that text has its own conventions of format and layout (**concepts about print**). These understandings are brought to the attention of early years specialists in the Desirable Outcomes document:

> They know that words and pictures carry meaning and that, in English, print is read from left to right and from top to bottom.

This awareness develops slowly during the early years when children are engaged in meaningful reading and writing activities that arise naturally at home, nursery and play group, often from a few months old. Sharing books and stories is, of course, central to this but so is making books, writing (and seeing written) letters, cards and notes. Young children being party to the use of print for all types of real-life purposes constantly reinforces the importance of being able to read and write. The use of commercially produced large texts and home-made 'big books' are invaluable for demonstrating to a small group of children that spoken language can be written down, that the marks and squiggles on the page always stand for the units of speech which can be read out, and for showing them where the print starts and ends and the direction in which it runs.

The symbolic nature of the alphabet

The next intellectual leap that children make is understanding that the letters of the alphabet are symbols and stand for the sounds they hear in speech. Through prolonged exposure to encounters with print the child's awareness becomes further refined to appreciate that these letters (or groups of letters) not only represent the sounds in speech but can also be put together to make up words and then sentences, which can be read to say something interesting or at least meaningful! This ability is highly predictive of success in reading once the child starts formal schooling. In a study I conducted on 191 new pupils, it was possible to predict with 80% accuracy which children would be reading by the end of their first year in the reception class from their entry assessments on admission to school (Riley, 1996). This skill is another of the statements in the Desirable Outcomes (1996) document:

> They recognise letters of the alphabet by shape and sound.

But only a rich, varied and meaningful programme of literacy activities will ensure that the child's knowledge of the alphabet is a genuinely valuable one and will promote the early stages of fluent reading. What is recognised is that simply teaching the alphabet to children is not an effective way to develop these understandings. Experiments in the US as long ago as the sixties produced results that were disappointing in the extreme. It would seem that young literacy learners develop competence most successfully through making their own connections when supported by an adult in the task of reading and writing. Direct teaching is useful only when it is grounded in an interesting activity with which the child is engaged.

The teaching of literacy through writing activities, books and stories

The stimulating nursery or playgroup environment provides a host of opportunities for the adult to model the use of written language as it naturally arises from activities and talking. Every early years classroom should include a designated space to be used for the teaching of literacy. Provide a writing area (or give a face-lift to an existing one e.g. card making, writing and posting) with all types of writing and mark-making implements and materials, pens, pencils, papers, envelopes, card, and ready-made blank booklets for writing stories and poems all enticingly presented and accessible. And also provide a quiet area furnished with cushions and carpet, containing a range of high quality books for browsing through and or sharing with an adult.

Adults need to demonstrate clearly the 'encoding' of speech into print by making books with and for children on a current pre-occupation or topic, writing letters, notes, lists, news, messages, rhymes and stories on white boards, on easels, in notebooks and on paper. After writing there follows the explicit 'decoding' back to the children, pointing to each word, with emphasis and clarity, as the message is read and re-read to make obvious the link between speech and text, sound and symbol.

It is preferable to display a frequently changing, smaller selection of interesting and challenging texts. All the books will have been chosen to represent a range of content, text features, illustrations and styles of writing. Large texts, both commercially produced and nursery-made, should be included. These books allow valuable literacy learning experience every time books are shared in a small group as they can be clearly seen and the way that print and its confusing conventions work can be reinforced. Pointing to the words as they are read aloud takes practice but is so facilitative that after several readings children will be joining in with the memorable phrases. Drawing attention to distinctive print features [e.g. Can anyone see a word that has the same ending/rhyme as this word?] highlights the important difference between a letter and a word and frequently repeated words focus children on the aspects of print to which they need to attend as they gradually develop understanding and competence.

Sharing story or non-fiction books is an opportunity for the adult to monitor this developing awareness of text and print. For example, do the children:

* listen attentively?

* talk and discuss effectively?

* follow the storyline?

* ask questions about the text?

* listen to and add to the contributions of others?

* show ability to predict what might happen next?

* offer alternative endings?

* have any appreciation of character and plot?

Certain essential understandings are needed by children if they are to be able to benefit from the more formal teaching of literacy they will experience in the reception class. These are usefully listed by Hall (1987, pp. 32-33):

* when we read we rely on print to carry the message

* print is different from pictures

- we read and use books in a particular order; from front to back

- we follow the print in a certain order: line by line, word by word

- books and print have a particular orientation

- print is made up of letters, words, punctuation and spaces

- there are relationships between words spoken and print observed and

- there is a language associated with the activity of reading books: front, back, page, word, letter, etc.

Early childhood educators can promote the development of these understandings whenever they work with children and so fully use the many situations that naturally arise in the nursery, reception or Year 1.

It has been suggested that pre-school children gradually acquire an overall knowledge of the purpose of print and how it represents spoken language, and an understanding also of the format of text and its particular conventions (**concepts about print**). This is the first layer of understanding that has to be acquired before progress in literacy can be made. The ways through which a deeper awareness of the features of print (**orthographic awareness**) and its relationship with sounds (**phonological awareness**) can also be developed, will be discussed later.

One aspect of the **'bottom-up skills'** is the concept that there is an alphabetic code and the important understanding that it is a symbolic system, and so represents the different sounds of spoken language in different and complex ways. The other aspect, as suggested earlier, of the 'bottom-up skills' is the ability to hear and distinguish the different sounds in words (phonological awareness) and to learn that these sounds can be mapped onto letters and groups of letters so as to read and write. The two abilities are related and they need to be taught both separately and jointly.

Developing print (orthographic) awareness
Sharing books, printed rhymes and poems provide many opportunities to focus on features of print.

The child demonstrates understanding by:

- saying for example 'I'll fetch the book about the big red bus!' thus indicating that he/she knows that the words in the title indicate the content of the book

- joining in with favourite stories i.e. understanding one-to-one correspondence of written and spoken words

- recognising and joining in with well known, often repeated parts of the text e.g. 'We're going on a bear hunt! It's going to be a big one!'

- pointing to specific and distinctive words as they are read

- knowing that Mum is a little word and Charlotte is a bigger word and neither is related to the size of the person they represent.

Environmental print can be capitalised upon to teach pupils the value of literacy and how print works.

The adults need to draw the children's attention to: labels, notices, instructions, packages and labels in the class shop or play corner, charts of helpers, days of the week, equipment, the words printed on the walls that are personally significant to individual pupils and the print in the outside environment by going for a 'looking-for-print-walk'.

The use of children's names can powerfully assist print awareness.

The adults in the playgroup or nursery can teach the alphabet by:

- substituting the names of characters in stories with the names of children in the group

- encouraging children to identify words that begin with the same letter of the alphabet as Darren's name etc

- writing captions under paintings e.g. 'Amanda has drawn her cat. Bill has painted his dumper truck'

- drawing children's attention to their friends' names with labels e.g. on coat pegs, shelves, pictures, models and belongings

- displaying a photo of each of the children, with name and what each likes doing and

- making books about the pupils and their favourite foods, activities e.g.

    William likes Cornflakes for breakfast;
    Sally likes Weetabix;
    Khadia likes Rice Krispies ...

Providing opportunities to write enables children to appreciate the links between speech and print.

Staff in the early years setting need to encourage the early writing of their pupils by:

- recognising when children demonstrate that they know the difference between drawing and writing

- responding to children's writing, making explicit what they know e.g. 'You are clever, you know that bus begins with a **b**'

- celebrating children's efforts by displaying their attempts

- sharing real writing with children e.g. letters, cards, notes, lists

- suggesting that children write for genuine purposes e.g. make a card for someone who is ill or for a birthday, making a list of cooking ingredients

- discussing the writing with children, point out print details, encourage them to read it

- encouraging the re-telling by drawing and/or writing a story

- making a class story for the wall – children do the illustrations/adult writes the text.

Developing sound (phonological) awareness

These understandings are again ones that adults working with the youngest children are encouraged to work towards. The SCAA guidelines say:

> They begin to associate sounds with patterns in rhymes, with syllables, and with words and letters.

Adults need to identify the children who are demonstrating an ability to begin to '**phonemically segment**' i.e. distinguish sounds within words. Children who are in the early stages of acquiring this crucial skill are able to discriminate aurally words that rhyme from one that does not e.g. h-**at**, c-**at**, r-**at**, h-**ad**; in the next stage they are able to supply a rhyming word with a word e.g. h-**en** *with* p-**en**. Next in the developmental sequence the children are able to differentiate between the words which begin with the same sound e.g. **m**-an, **m**-ad, **m**-en, **p**-en. Finally, and after some experience of reading, they can split a word into its component sounds or phonemes e.g. **ch-ick-en.**

The children in the nursery or playgroup need to experience:

- a variety of rhymes and verses, learning them by heart and matching spoken word to printed word

- a poem or rhyme of the week printed on the easel, for reading and re-reading, chanting

- sharing 'big books' with distinctively patterned and rhyming text. Several readings are valuable reinforcement and provide the opportunity to join in

- supplying a string of words that rhyme with a particular word during writing or reading activities, e.g. **rod, pod, cod, tod, hod**. Even thinking of nonsense words can be fun and they emphasise that language is a flexible system

- opportunities to break words into the beginning and end sounds e.g. **M-um, b-ook**, particularly when writing and

- activities such as the game 'I spy' and 'All those with a name beginning with **T** can fetch their snack'.

The following stage of print and sound awareness is developed through activities such as the adult explicitly mapping the sound (**phoneme**) onto the written symbol (**grapheme**), when writing the daily message or sentence for the group. Children master the inconsistencies and vagaries of the English alphabetical system if given the appropriate experiences, support and encouragement. Early childhood staff working with young children use praise effectively to encourage early attempts, make explicit to the learners what they know and provide further opportunities for them to progress. Very young children working and playing in this type of setting will be 'scaffolded' into developing as speakers and listeners, readers and writers.

Research findings are indicating the importance of the first years of education. A successful early start to formal learning prepares children for everything school has to offer, and these are the children who make the most academic progress throughout their educational careers. Adults working in early years settings have both the opportunity and responsibility to affect the future learning of their pupils in a far-reaching and powerful way.

Useful addresses

Books for Keeps (Children's book magazine. Published 6 times a year, obtainable by subscription only)
6, Brightfield Road, Lee
London SE.12 8QF

Madeleine Lindley (Books for Children and their Teachers)
Book Centre
Broadgate, Broadway Business Park,
Chadderton,

Oldham OL9 9XA
Tel.0161-683-4400
Fax.0161-682-6801

Language Matters Journal of the Centre for Language in Primary Education.
Published 3 times a year. (Subscription includes CLPE library membership)
CLPE
London Borough of Southwark
Webber Row
London SE1 8QW

References

Adams, M. J. (1990) *Beginning to Read: Thinking and Learning about Print* Cambridge, Mass: MIT Press

Cummins, J. (1978) 'Linguistic interdependence and the educational development of bilingual children'. *Review of Educational Research*, Vol. 49, pp. 222-51

Cummins, J. (1984a) *Bilingualism and Special Education: Issues in Assessment and Pedagogy*, Clevedon: Multilingual Matters

DES (1989) *Aspects of Primary Education: The Education of Children under Five*, London: HMSO

Donaldson, M. (1978) *Children's Minds*, Glasgow: Collins

Donaldson, M.(1989) *Sense and Sensibility: Some Thoughts on the Teaching of Literacy* (Occasional Paper 3), Reading: Reading and Language Centre, University of Reading

Hall, N. (1987) *The Emergence of Literacy*, Sevenoaks: Hodder and Stoughton

ILEA (1990b) *Language and Power*, London: Harcourt Brace Jovanovitch

Riley, J.L. (1996) *The Teaching of Reading: The Development of Literacy in the Early Years of School,* London: Paul Chapman

SCAA (1996) *Nursery Education Desirable Outcomes for Children's Learning on entering compulsory education.* London: DfEE

CHAPTER 4

DOING MATHEMATICS WITH YOUNG CHILDREN

Patti Barber

Introduction

Thinking about numeracy in the early years has recently changed (Hughes, 1986, Aubrey, 1994, Munn, 1997) and this has had a direct bearing on what we need to provide in the early years setting for mathematics. Since the publication of the Desirable Outcomes (SCAA, 1996) for children starting school, far more emphasis has been put on the development of basic skills in the early years, including mathematics.

> These outcomes cover important aspects of mathematical understanding and provide the foundation for numeracy. They focus on achievement through practical activities and on using and understanding language in the development of simple mathematical ideas. (SCAA, 1996)

Key points emerge from recent research:

- Traditional views on teaching numeracy based on Piagetian theory are doubted

- A counting-based skills curriculum should underpin numeracy

- Activities should be based in familiar contexts

- Counting should include large numbers

- Traditional expectations of what children can do may have been inaccurate

- Vygotskian theory supports 'good early years' practice'.

Number

Mathematics is more than just number, but number is a very important aspect. Developing number understanding gives opportunities to develop wider aspects of mathematics such as pattern spotting, abstract thinking and problem solving. In the 1960s and 1970s early years education was heavily influenced by attempts to apply Piaget's developmental theory to the learning of mathematics. Among the important ideas in his writing is the concept of conservation. It has had immense impact on the teaching of early number, translated in the early years classroom as activities about matching, sorting and classifying. Researchers (Davies, 1991; Clements, 1983), however, have questioned the emphasis in the early years on number activities drawn from 'Piagetian concepts' (pre-number activities based on logical operations, as below). Davies (1991) points out that Piaget himself did not draw implications for the curriculum from his theories and argues that tasks of conservation are a misapplication of his work.

Clements (1983) compared different approaches to teaching number. One group was taught classifying and ordering (logical operations), the second was taught counting skills (number concepts) and the third was a control group. Tests of 'number concepts' and 'logical operations' were given as pre- and post-tests to all three groups. The 'number' and 'logical' groups performed better than the control group in both post-tests but the number group did significantly better in the number test than either of the other groups. The implication was that the counting skills approach and not the logical operations led to higher skills of numeracy.

In Aubrey's study (1994) children who had no formal experience of sorting, classifying, ordering, matching (one-to-one correspondence) or mapping activities showed an unexpectedly high level of understanding of number in a reception class where they had been for only two weeks.

So are activities based on sorting, conservation, classification, matching and one-to-one correspondence helpful in promoting an early understanding of number? Theories point to a 'counting skills' approach to early number as being more successful overall than a more 'traditional logical operations' (Piagetian) approach, for example, encouraging children to count with a purpose, such as the candles on a birthday cake.

Counting

'There is little doubt that children's understanding of number is rooted in counting' (Maclellan, 1997). It appears that many children begin counting from early on and have fairly sophisticated understandings when they reach reception classes (Aubrey, 1994) but still need considerable adult support. Research (Maclellan, 1997) suggests that children need to count in many differing contexts to develop their skills and that counting has to have a purpose (Munn, 1997). Carr *et al* (1991) emphasise a range of purposes for number use. The purpose of counting must be explicit for children. If adults are seen counting out loud for a reason (counting the numbers of children for dinners, say,) children have more readily grasp the mental aspect of the activity that they see (Munn, 1997). Donaldson (1979) discusses the influence of context in allowing young children access to mathematical problems.

Cowan and Ewers-Rogers (1996) found that young children revealed a remarkable range of knowledge about numbers and everyday practices involving them. They know that numbers are not used just to represent quantities. Maclellan (1997) described the work of Fuson and Hall (1983), who listed at least six types of context in which pre-school children might experience number words:

- sequence (number words said in order but not counting anything)

- counting (number words are tagged to objects)

- cardinal (number word signifies the numerosity)

- measure (number words apply to the numerosity of the units of measure)

- non-numerical (number words are a name or code)

We need to ensure that very young children are provided with practical addition and subtraction experiences, such as using pennies when shopping or playing games that involve taking or winning a number of objects according to the throw of a die, and to take care not to formalise the activities too early (Aubrey, 1997) using abstract symbols. Children's interest in large numbers needs to be encouraged (Gifford, 1995). Gifford's research shows that children of three and four can count large numbers of objects, as well as reciting long number sequences and being able to write two digit numbers. Some can even calculate with numbers up to ten and know some number facts such as 8 and 8 is 16 and a million is more than a thousand. There has been an increasing body of research illustrating young children's possession of many and complex abilities (Aubrey, 1994, Donaldson,, 1978, Hughes,1986).

Another reason for encouraging counting of numbers beyond 20 is our idiosyncratic system of number names. Children in Japan, Taiwan and Korea consistently fared better in international tests than British and American (US) children. One significant factor may be the names given to our numbers. After learning the counting number names to ten in the English system there are the unusual names of eleven, twelve, thirteen, etc., whereas in the Japanese system eleven is ten one, twelve is ten two. When the Japanese reach twenty this is two ten and ninety-nine is the equivalent of nine ten nine. As Thompson (1997) observed:

> The structure can therefore be seen to be highly regular, logical and systematic, and such consistency and regularity must surely facilitate the appreciation and absorption of the recurring pattern that underlies this counting system.

The problem in English is exacerbated by the different spellings and pronunciations of ten; we have endings of *teen* and *ty*. In Japanese ten is used as ten in all these instances. And confusion can arise from the representation of the teens numbers. Even though we say six before the ten in sixteen, we then proceed to write the number as 16, with the teen before the six. It is not surprising that children reverse the digits in the teens numbers when they first write them down.

Children find difficulty working with abstract symbols in mathematics (Hughes, 1986) and it is sometimes hard to create meaningful experiences. But there are many opportunities to pursue in the role-play area, for example, making supermarket bills or lists. It is important for children to have experience of numerals in a meaningful context, for example, stock check when tidying-up: 4 pencils, 5 erasers.

Other areas of mathematics

Underlying good early years practice are the theories of Vygotsky, which emphasise a much greater role for the adult and/or knowledgeable 'other' in the development of the child. He stresses the importance of interaction, communication and instruction in the development of understanding, as discussed in Chapter 1. Problem solving needs to be encouraged and built into as many tasks as possible. For example, how can we plant these six bulbs in two pots? In **geometry** (shape and space) it is important to find out what children come to school understanding. Aubrey (1994) found in her study that 4 year-old children bring into school an ability to sort and classify two and three dimensional shapes, build complex 3-D constructions, draw two dimensional shapes and use common words to describe position in space and on a line. Piaget and Inhelder (1969 cited in Aubrey, 1997) implied that children aged 3 and 4 deal with the topological (where things are in relation to each other in space) aspects of geometry and then move onto curved and straight-sided aspects of shape at 4 to 6 years. The language of shape and space is paramount in the learning of geometry.

Much of the research literature concerning **measurement** is drawn from Piagetian theory. Very early on children understand about 'bigger than', for instance, in terms of food and their own portion. Evidence shows that children bring to school a range of strategies for solving simple mathematical problems, based on everyday encounters involving measurement. They will have seen their parents or carers looking at clocks to time things, or setting timers on microwave ovens or video recorders. However, children need time to understand the key ideas underpinning measures: the concepts of transitivity and conservation. The concept of conservation relates to the idea that quantities stay the same despite changes in appearance. So the amount of liquid poured into a new and different shaped container remains the same. An understanding of transitivity is based on dealing with units, where a third item is used indirectly to compare two things. For example, if a bean growing in a pot is as long as a particular stick, and the stick is moved next to a growing flower which is found to be the same height, then the bean and the flower must be the same height.

Concepts of **data handling** and reasoning need to be supported in the early years by recording data with children in as many ways as possible. Using an event such as the birth of hamsters can trigger all sorts of recording. How much do they weigh? How much have they grown? It is helpful to use a range of diagrams and not just block graphs. Carroll diagrams are helpful in an 'Ourselves' project, as shown below:

A Carroll diagram representing eye and hair colour

	Eye colour-brown	Eye colour-blue
Hair colour-dark	Julie	Penny
	Tara	Eve
	Charlie	Crystal
hair colour-fair	George	Mark
	John	Junior
	Dwayne	Zara

Questions can then be posed about the diagram: who has fair hair and brown eyes? dark hair and brown eyes?

Promoting learning in mathematics

Learning mathematics can be promoted through a mathematically rich environment. This can be achieved through what we say and do and also through what we provide.

The first aspect is provided through mathematical language, the importance of which is discussed further on.

Small children should be provided with access to mathematical equipment such as calculators, large handleable numbers, dice, dominoes, construction materials, 2-D and 3-D shapes. Mathematical instruments such as weighing scales, clocks, calendars and watches, rulers, tape measures, height charts, games and puzzles should also be available. Logic and reasoning can be encouraged through the organisation of the materials. For example, one early years setting has all the construction materials sorted into types and labelled with relevant pictures and a geometric shape. When the children tidy up they learn that each set of equipment has one place where it is stored and this is based on a specific criterion (matching the shape on the box of equipment to the shape on the cupboard). This enables children to begin to use logical systems on a daily basis for a purpose. Based on this criterion, children are able to reason where things belong and tidy up accordingly. Their bricks and lego are also arranged in logical groupings.

A positive climate for learning

Two vital aspects of creating a positive climate are intrinsically connected and will be discussed together. They are:

* to adopt a positive ethos concentrating on what children know as they come into the early years setting and use this as a starting point

* to bridge the gap between what happens at home and at school. (Sylva and Siraj-Blatchford, 1996)

Home learning differs from school learning. Home learning can be comfortable, allow plenty of space for incidental learning and be rich and responsive to language development. Children who have much experience of everyday mathematics will begin to use the language of mathematics before they start school. As important concepts develop, children will begin to reflect on and talk about mathematical aspects of familiar situations.

When these children enter school it is often hard to see the links between home and school mathematics. The knowledge children bring with them from home is often underestimated by teachers, who assume that they have little understanding of mathematics and begin with the simplest concepts.

Research (Munn, 1997) shows that mathematics content is often minimal in activities in early years settings – generally far less than children would be receiving in a stimulating home environment.

Problems

There is no concrete focus for maths activity as in literacy

Early years settings seldom offer a focus for mathematics that comes near to matching print as a focus for learning to read. As maths is a mental activity children can not easily recognise what they are doing. For example, discovering the capacities of saucepans and jugs in the water tray is a common mathematical activity but there is no guarantee that a child will focus on which jug holds the most water. Compared with literacy activities, which can take up to almost half a child's playing time, mathematics activities seem to occupy a fleeting and incidental position in children's everyday lives.

There are ideas in literacy that we might imitate in mathematics, for example, the popular and successful 'PACT' folders for reading at home. The mathematical equivalent is often to take home a 'maths game' to play. (IMPACT (1988) is a series of home activities in mathematics devised by Ruth Merttens).

Stories themselves are good ways of promoting aspects of mathematics. *The Doorbell Rang*, for example, is based around the multiples of twelve. I have seen young children sharing out twelve biscuits in several different groupings based on the story. Stories such as *Jim and the Beanstalk* can inspire a topic on giants where measurement can be explored through discussion on relative size and comparison. This story encourages children to role-play and creates a world where things are 'bigger than' themselves. It also provides experience of using large numbers when, for example, measuring the giant. A topic on 'Ourselves' lends itself to a wide range of mathematically based activities.

Encourage children to make a book of their own 'special' numbers – their age, door number, the number of the bus to granny's house, their shoe size. Encourage them to talk about the number of brothers, sisters or pets they have at home. As part of the topic children can weigh themselves and measure their height and use height charts to see how much each has grown over time. The Desirable Outcomes (SCAA,1996) state that children should be familiar with number rhymes, stories, counting games and activities.

Some number rhymes work well with a large group focusing on mental mathematics, such as *The five little speckled frogs*. Ask children how many frogs are on the log when two have jumped off and let them show the number with their fingers or a wooden numeral.

Adults are often not confident about the maths curriculum for pre-school children

Mathematics has traditionally been a subject that intimidates many people. Although the confident practitioner is able to determine and extend children's learning in mathematics, there are many adults who do not find this easy. Hannah, age 3, was counting how many balloons she had to fill – 'It's 1, 2, 4, 5, 2. I've got 2 to fill'. It can be unnerving to be faced with a child who cannot recite the number names in order and then gives the wrong amount at the end. What should the adult do next? Adults working with young children need to be aware of the complexities associated with counting and have the knowledge to extend children's mathematical thinking.

Not all children learn counting in the same order but a suggested progression is that they:

* learn the first few number names in the right order (followed perhaps by random numbers such as 1,2,3,4,5,6,7,9,11,14,.......)

* say one number for one object counted without missing one or repeating any

* understand that the last number you say tells you how many there are

* get a feel for estimating quantities by looking at the pattern of objects (e.g. dots on dice)

* learn more number names in order and can say what number comes next without going back to the beginning each time

* use stories and rhymes to count backwards from 0 to 5

* use ordinal number names (e.g. first, second, third)

(Adapted from *Number in the Nursery and Reception*, 1998)

Inservice support can help adults working with young children. Gifford *et al* (1995) found in their study that number did not have a high priority in the nursery at the beginning of their project but once staff were aware they developed many opportunities for children. Another crucial part of the adult's role in the early years setting is to help children develop positive attitudes to mathematics. This means that the adult needs to value the experiences and knowledge children bring to the nursery and to develop a partnership with parents and carers. Also we need to show how we use mathematics in our daily lives and share this with children. If adults refer regularly to numbers on clocks, calendars, registers and measures, then children can begin to appreciate the different purposes and meanings of number.

Mathematical ability

Children's ability varies widely so we cannot generalise about the mathematics experience they need. Before offering an appropriate curriculum we must understand a child's capabilities in mathematics. Observing children in their play is a starting point for planning mathematically based activities. Each child has had different experiences, which means that all have their own starting points and needs. It is important also to get a feel for the children's experience of home life to recognise the influences in their learning.

If numbers are put on familiar objects from home in the home corner, then children can relate their home experiences of number and measurement to the nursery environment.

Providing relevant activities in mathematics

Planning

Make sure that planning is appropriate for individual children through concerted observation and knowledge of the child's previous experiences. Describing 4 year-old children's abilities in geometry Aubrey (1994) points out that 'such responses (it's flat, it's round....) demonstrate the need for the teacher to listen, discuss and question individual children to assess existing experiences and vocabulary and to enrich and extend this.' The topic of Giants, as referred to earlier, has the potential for a tremendous amount of mathematics. Activities and discussions could include the following:

- Build large constructions for the giant's house

- Fill big pots for the giant's tea. Why does the giant need a large cup? Does it hold more than your cup at home?

- Make giant sandwiches using French loaves with different fillings. Could you eat such a big sandwich?

- Compare well-known objects by size. Is the giant larger than a house or smaller than a bus? What are you bigger than?

- Compare the objects by weight. Does the giant weigh more than the bus?

- Set up the home corner as a giant's house, with everything as large as possible

- Make ten different giants out of paper or junk materials and order them by height

- Discuss how old the giant is. Can giants be young?

- Compare clothing sizes. If a child is size 5, what size is the giant? What sizes do adults have on their clothing?

- Discuss big numbers. Where do you see big numbers? On buses? On door numbers?

Looking at Children's Learning SCAA (1997) highlights ways of integrating the Desirable Outcomes (SCAA, 1996) into planning in the early years and suggests interesting activities analysed in terms of their learning outcomes.

Activities need to be in familiar contexts

According to Fuson and Hall (1983), any number word is, initially, learned as several different words, each of which is tied to the context in which it is used e.g. child's age, door number, time to go to school. With repeated use, the different nuances of meaning are seen to be related to each other and so children learn that there are various meanings for any one number word. Donaldson (1979) argues that teachers have underestimated the rational powers of young children and ignored the importance of context in interpreting the meaning of what children say. Educators need to present mathematics that gives children opportunities to show that they understand the problem. Presenting activities in familiar contexts helps to alleviate the gap between home and school learning.

Routines are a useful way of developing mathematics on a regular basis. Tidying up can provide opportunities to develop mathematical understanding. Simple timing devices (such as wind-up toys, egg timers, tocker timers) can be used to see how long the routine takes. Early recognition of the need to classify data can be encouraged through the use of systems of storage (putting all the same shaped bricks together, all the lego windows separately from the wheels). Having children check the number of pencils and erasers carefully encourages counting and using numbers with a purpose. Tidy lists can stimulate their interest in and recognition of symbols.

Role-play is a rich source to build children's confidence to make mathematical marks. A post office offers a wide range of tasks to encourage writing symbols, such as writing their own numbers on stamps and postal orders. A successful topic about travel culminated in children numbering airline seats in a role-play area converted into an aeroplane. They numbered the seats up to surprisingly high numbers, had discussions about speed and distance and counted down to zero, thus showing competence beyond traditionally accepted limits of achievement (Gifford, 1995).

Language needs to be appropriate to the children's level

Mathematical language is an important part of language acquisition. It is crucial to mathematical thinking and it allows children to talk precisely about their experiences and to reflect upon them. Mathematical language involves everyday words used in a precise and particular way. For example, *half* in everyday speech means two parts that are roughly the same size. In mathematical terminology half means that the two pieces are exactly the same size.

Mathematical language needs to be developed in the early years and aspects to be included are:

- Knowing the names (of shapes for example). Once a child is familiar with a cube then all the properties of that shape are drawn together under one name

- Knowing the vocabulary of relationships e.g. shape, size, position and quantity. Without this language children would not be able to describe 'bigger than', 'more than' etc

- Using questions to express their curiosity, 'What would happen if...'

- Predicting and hypothesising as important aspects of the mathematical thought process. Children need to learn to answer such questions as 'Why do you think the blocks fit better this way?'

(Adapted from *Learning Mathematics in the Nursery: Desirable Approaches*, 1997).

An understanding of the link between activity and language development on the subject of shape and space is important but it is easier to understand the value of learning number. Through early childhood experiences children encounter natural shapes and constructed shapes, they develop an awareness of colour, form and texture and, through their own mobility, they explore position in space. These experiences form the basis for later description in more precise mathematical language of shape and space.

The language of measurement can be encouraged by adults using the appropriate language when estimating and comparing e.g. Is it bigger? Does it weigh more? A wide range of activities should be provided, so that all aspects of measurement are explored (volume, capacity, time, temperature, length and weight). Appropriate activities can encourage a wealth of language. Take for example bathing dolls: discussions can centre on the amount of water in the doll's bath or what happens to the water when the doll is put in or pulled out. Why does the surface level of water rise? What happens when you get into the bath?

Activities need to be open-ended

To be able to cope with the wide range of experiences that children have in their early years, activities need to be open-ended and allow for extension for the more able. When planning, adults need to make sure that extension activities are thought through so that if children can work out a simple number pattern they can move on to ideas that lead on from it. In the shoe shop, for instance, the first activity would be a straight comparison of 'Who has the longest foot?' The next activity could involve using a foot measurer. So providing an extension for children who made the comparisons easily by allowing them to begin measuring for themselves.

Interactive games can help to introduce the language of mathematics

Games that assist counting are jumping games (e.g. hopscotch), throwing beanbags (counting how many landed in the bucket), and counting people by touching them (simple 'tag' games). Rhymes, songs, stories and games all appeal to young children and are an unpressurised link between home and school. One way of involving children in mathematical language is to set up repetitive activities that require a stereotyped 'response' from the child. As babies learn the rules of conversation by starting with turn-taking games, so older children can learn the rules of mathematical language by starting with repetitive interactive games e.g. moving on in board games.

Examples of appropriate activities in familiar contexts

The Home Corner becomes a hospital

Give children opportunities to use thermometers under close adult supervision. Many children will have had their temperature taken at home or at the doctors. The aims of this activity would be to develop the language of temperature – is it high? low? What does this mean? And to use large numbers in a context of measurement and to encourage children to record their findings.

Adults would need to provide information about the body's normal temperature and why it needs to be measured. When else we would use temperature gauges (e.g. on a cooker, a greenhouse, central heating thermostat)? Discuss how the information about patients is collected in hospital and then make boards for charts in the home corner. Children should be observed to see if they discuss differences in their temperatures and how they choose to record the information. An extension for the children who show an understanding of temperature is to explore finding the temperature of cold things e.g. cold water with ice in it.

The Sand Tray – Sand Drawing

Encourage children to draw lines and shapes with forks in the sand tray and describe them. Talk about whether the lines are straight or curved, what shapes are between the lines and what difference it would make to use a stick instead of a fork. Observation of the children should focus on the language they use e.g. words to describe their lines, such as curvy and pointy. Do they identify any shapes they have made? And do they use words like up or down? Extensions could include making 3-D shapes, naming shapes and creating sand designs on card.

Outdoor play – The Hopping Line

Painting or chalking a number line on an outside area can provide opportunities for many different activities. Games such as hopping from one numeral to the next while saying each number will help children to remember the order of the numerals. Things to discuss would be: What other games do you play with numbers printed on the ground e.g. hopscotch, snakes and ladders. What number do you start on? How many hops does it take to get from 1 to 2? Observe whether the children say the number words in sequence as they hop? Do they talk about the numerals, recognise them or read them out? Or try to predict what number their next hop will land them on? Extensions could be developing a hopping line pattern where the adult devises a pattern, calls out the numbers and gets the children to follow her pattern exactly.

Contexts that children know and enjoy

Parties

Involving children in preparing for parties in different forms and contexts gives valuable experience of putting mathematics to real use. All aspects of mathematics can be covered. Many celebrations are appropriate for a party e.g. a range of festivals, individual birthdays or a party for the teddy bears.

Voting

Encourage the children to vote for different options for food and games. For example 'Which flavour of cake would you like?' There are different ways of recording the children's choices. They can tick a picture of the cake, or each child can draw their favourite choice and stick this underneath a picture of the appropriate cake. Children can be observed to see if they count the votes and say how many there are. Do they read the numerals? Do they make comparisons? Extensions about food could be working out how many different sandwiches can be made using combinations of two breads and spreads.

Drinks

Aspects of measurement can be explored by working out how much juice is needed for a party. Children can work out how many litres will be needed for the whole group by pouring the same measured amount into a number of glasses that have different shapes but the same capacity. Fairness needs to be discussed and how to make sure that each child gets the same amount. The adult needs to check that the children understand how to measure cupfuls from a bottle and how to make sure there is enough. Observation should focus on whether the correct language is used, e.g. my glass is wide/narrow. Do any of the children realise that differently shaped glasses can hold the same amount?

Hats

Making different shaped hats, simple crowns, triangular and conical hats, gives children experience of the change from 2-D to 3-D. It is important to establish why some shapes are more appropriate for hats e.g. cones and cylinders. What do the shapes look like flat? Can children predict what a hat will look like? Observe the children to see if they choose the right shapes to fold and fit together. Do the children use the appropriate language e.g. round, pointed, rectangle, cone?

Activities adapted from *Nursery Mathematics* (Barber, Gifford and Munn, 1997)

How can we assess these activities?

Observation and careful monitoring

Observing children and seeing what they do in a range of contexts seems essential if we are to follow their interests and build on their ways of learning. Recording the observations is important and children should be encouraged to record for themselves. This enables the adult to monitor progress and pick up clues to the child's thinking. Attitudes to mathematics also need to be noted. Gifford (1994) found that some young children were anxious about numbers. Children need to be encouraged to use numbers in familiar settings and within an early years setting with a positive approach to mathematics. This points to the need to monitor attitudes and aim consciously to keep confidence and interest high.

In all areas of mathematics (number, shape and space, measures and data handling) children bring into school a rich informal knowledge learned in everyday situations (Aubrey1994) and it is a part of the nursery practitioner's task to tap into this knowledge.

Asking the right questions

Questions should be as encouraging and as challenging as possible. Children need opportunities to express themselves and describe what they think and see. A challenging question for a four-year-old is one that requires initiative when answering it. Try 'what do you see when I say six?' Or make it more difficult by asking 'Imagine six buttons and move them around. Can you imagine them in two groups? How many buttons are in each group?' Children need to get used to being asked questions and they need time to think and reflect about their answers. Avoid questions to which the answer is too obvious. A thought-provoking question might be 'What did you learn today?' Reflective questions need careful timing as we cannot always reflect on something that has just taken place. Pertinent questions can be used to extend learning, for example 'How could we record our votes?', and to assess how much knowledge children already have. Appropriate questioning can enhance the learning of the adult and the children.

There are many issues to be considered when providing mathematical experiences for young children and we should always remember that young children learn most of their early mathematics at home and that they struggle to link their home/school experiences. The early years setting is the place which should supply the appropriate curriculum where children can move from their home learning into preparing for the more formal curriculum of the future.

Recommended texts to support mathematics planning in the early years

Barber, P., Gifford, S. and Munn, P. (1997) *Nursery Mathematics.* London: Heinemann
A useful set of activities covering a wide range of mathematics in the early years and providing assessments, extensions and appropriate language to use.

Cook, G., Jones, L., Murphy, C., and Thumpston. G. (1997) *Enriching Early Mathematical Learning*. Buckingham: Open University Press
Interesting activities and extensions that are discussed in considerable detail.

The Early Childhood Mathematics Group (1997) *Learning Mathematics in the Nursery: Desirable Approaches*. London: BEAM
A useful expansion of the SCAA Desirable Outcomes and ways to integrate these into a sound early years curriculum.

Thompson, I. (ed.) (1997) *Teaching and Learning Early Number.* Buckingham: Open University Press
A wealth of knowledge based on recent research focusing on number.

References

Aubrey, C. (1994) An Investigation of Children's knowledge of Mathematics at School Entry and the Knowledge their Teachers hold about Teaching and Learning Mathematics, about Young Learners and Mathematical Subject Knowledge. *British Educational Research Journal* Vol. 20 no. 1 1994. pp 105-120

Aubrey, C. (1997) *Mathematics Teaching in the Early Years*. London: Falmer Press

Barber, P., Gifford, S. and Munn, P.(1997) *Nursery Mathematics*. London: Heinemann

Carr, M., Peters, S. and Young-Loveridge, J. (1991) *The Informal Mathematics of Four year-olds: Understanding Its Purpose*. New Zealand: University of Waikato

Davies, A. (1991) Piaget, Teachers and Education: into the 1990s. In Light, P., Sheldon, S. and Woodhead, M. (1991) *Learning to Think*. London: Routledge

Donaldson, M. (1979) *Children's Minds*. London: Fontana

Ewers-Rogers, J. and Cowan, R. (1996) Children as Apprentices to Number. In *Early Child Development and Care* 1996 Vol.125 pp

Fuson, K. and Hall, J. (1983) The Acquisition of Early Number Word Meanings. In Ginsburg, H. (ed.), *The Development of Mathematical Thinking*. London: Academic Press

Gifford, S. (1995) Number in Early Childhood. *Early Child Development and Care* Vol. 109. pp 95-119

Gifford, S. (1998) *Number in the Nursery and Reception*. BEAM: London

Hughes, M. (1986) *Children and Number*. Oxford: Blackwell

Hutchins, P. (1986) *The Doorbell Rang*. London: Puffin

Maclellan, E. (1997) The importance of counting. In Thompson, I. (ed.) (1997) *Teaching and Learning Early Number*. Buckingham: Open University Press

Merttens, R. and Vass, J. (ed.) (1993) *Partnership in Maths*. London: Falmer Press.

Munn, P. (1997) Children's beliefs about counting. In Thompson, I. (ed.) (1997) *Teaching and Learning Early Number*. Buckingham: Open University Press

SCAA (1996) *Desirable Outcomes for Children's Learning*. London: DFEE

SCAA (1997) *Looking at Children's Learning*. London: DFEE

Sylva, K. and Siraj-Blatchford, I.(1996) *Bridging the Gap between Home and School*. Paris: UNESCO

The Early Childhood Mathematics Group (1997) *Learning Mathematics in the Nursery: Desirable Approaches*. London: BEAM

Thompson, I. (1997) The Early Years Number Curriculum. In Thompson (ed.) *Teaching and Learning Early Number*. Buckingham: Open University Press

Williams, H. (1996) Developing Numeracy in the Early Years. In Merttens, R. (ed.) *Teaching Numeracy – maths in the classroom*. Leamington Spa: Scholastic

CHAPTER 5

SCIENCE IN THE EARLY YEARS
Esmé Glauert

Introduction

This chapter examines the nature of science in the early years and current thinking about learning science. Strategies that can be used to promote children's scientific development and create a positive climate for learning are outlined and ways of resourcing and organising science experiences considered.

What do we mean by science in the early years?

Science in the early years seeks to extend children's knowledge and understanding of the physical and biological world and to help them develop more effective, systematic ways of finding out. Everyday play activities and the immediate environment offer rich opportunities for learning and for capitalising on young children's interest in the world around them. For example, through cooking and making activities children can begin to learn about materials and their properties and appropriate safety precautions. Observing and looking after plants and animals can enhance their understanding about what is needed for life and encourage respect for living things. Outdoor play provides a wealth of opportunities for making things move and experiencing forces. The task of the adult is to identify the scientific potential in these activities and to build upon it.

Science can make a number of contributions to the early years curriculum. Aims for science with young children include:

* fostering and building on children's ideas and interests

* increasing children's understanding of their physical and biological environments and their place within them

- promoting an awareness of science in everyday life

- helping children in their interactions with the world, for example in relation to health and safety, making things work or caring for living things

- stimulating critical thinking, respect for evidence and concern for the environment

- developing positive attitudes and approaches to learning and supporting pupils in learning how to learn and

- providing a basis for future science learning.

These aims reflect important principles in early years practice, building on young children's capabilities, developing positive attitudes and approaches to learning and providing an education that is helpful and relevant to children in their lives at present.

Key areas of development in science are as follows:

Knowledge and understanding of scientific concepts

Science seeks to develop children's knowledge and understanding in relation to: living things and their environment; materials and their properties; and physical processes – electricity, magnetism, sound, light, forces, and earth in space.

Skills, processes and procedural understanding related to scientific enquiry

Science provides opportunities for developing *skills* associated with scientific enquiry such as using equipment, measuring or using tables to record results. Younger children will need the help of an adult.

Scientific processes are used in developing and testing ideas. These include:

observing	grouping, classifying, looking for similarities and differences
raising questions	identifying scientific questions, raising questions that can be investigated
predicting	using previous knowledge and experience and patterns in observations
hypothesising	offering tentative explanations
investigating	testing out ideas, identifying variables, beginning to recognise the need for a fair test, starting to use measurement
interpreting	finding patterns in results, drawing conclusions, suggesting relationships
communicating	discussing, making records in a variety of ways, communicating findings

evaluating   evaluating approaches used or how far the conclusions
support initial ideas

As children gain in experience they begin to develop an understanding of scientific procedures – how to put together process skills and existing knowledge and understanding in solving a problem: for example, developing an understanding of the need for a fair test or appreciating the importance of care in taking measurements.

These skills and processes are not unique to science but are important in learning across the curriculum. There are strong connections with measurement in mathematics and aspects of speaking and listening in language.

Attitudes in science

Attitudes and personal qualities play a vital role in learning. Making a good start depends on promoting positive and confident *attitudes to science* and fostering *scientific attitudes* such as curiosity, flexibility, respect for evidence, critical reflection, sensitivity to the living and non-living environment. Curiosity is a key starting point for learning. It is vital that children's questions are taken seriously and that they are encouraged to ask questions by seeing adults adopting a questioning approach to the world around them. Being prepared to change ideas and approaches, looking critically at evidence and learning from mistakes are all important in science learning. Many experiences in science provide opportunities for children to learn to respect living and non-living things and to consider the effects of their actions on the environment. Science also provides valuable opportunities for developing attitudes and personal qualities conducive to learning across the curriculum such as co-operation, perseverance and a willingness to ask questions.

Ideas about science and scientists

Through the experiences provided for young children we contribute implicitly or explicitly to their views about science and its links with society and everyday life. Even young children have been shown to have stereotyped views of scientists – white, male, western, and often weird looking – and to have a limited view of science as an activity (see for example, Smail, 1993). Introducing a range of people engaged in scientific activity or who use science in their work, making the most of books or visits, highlighting links between science, technology and everyday life, for example in relation to electricity or medicines, or discussing areas where children can begin to take responsibility in their lives such as rubbish disposal or caring for living things might help to broaden children's views of science and indicate its relevance to their lives.

What do we know about children's learning in science?

The following examples will help illustrate a number of characteristics of young children's learning.

Example 1: Sophie's boat for Max (age 5:4)

The children had been reading the story *Where the Wild Things Are* by Maurice Sendak. In the story the child Max has a dream in which he sails off in a magic boat to where the Wild Things are. Several children had tried different ways of making boats out of various materials. Sophie made a boat out of lego. She was very surprised when it floated for a while, then it tipped forward and gradually sank. Over the next couple of days she made several boats, changing the height of the sides, the shape of the front and the base and the distribution of the blocks round the side. She explored ways of blocking up the gaps.

Example 2: Washing the dolls' clothes (age 4)

The nursery staff had suggested that the dolls' clothes needed washing so Nargis and Sam took a bundle to the sink and covered them with water. They tried scrubbing and squeezing the clothes.

Sam observed: 'the water's changed colour, it's going mucky.'

Nargis said: 'The red (paint stain), it's melting off.'

After a while, they noticed that not all the clothes were coming clean.

Building on these observations the nursery staff planned a series of follow-up activities: carrying out investigations to see if adding soap or warm water made the clothes cleaner, exploring what happened to various substances in water – oil, paint, glue, mud, sand.

Example 3: Visiting the Baby Clinic

After work on growth and keeping healthy, a reception class took their dolls and teddies to a local baby clinic. The local health visitor had agreed to take part in a role-play where the children acted the role of parents bringing their children to the clinic. Their 'children' were examined and health visitors asked the 'parents' if they had any problems and gave advice about health matters. At the end of the visit the class asked the health visitors about their jobs and what they needed to know to do their work (first reported in Sherrington, 1993).

Example 4: Eye colour (age 4:2) A parent's report of a conversation

Situation	It was bedtime
Child	Why does Daddy, James (big brother), and me have blue eyes and you have green eyes?
Parent	(Told her she got her eyes from Daddy. Then said goodnight and left the room.)
Child	(child calls mother back 5 minutes later) I like Pee Wee Herman and I have blue eyes. Daddy likes Pee Wee Herman and he has blue eyes. James likes Pee Wee Herman and he has blue eyes. If you like Pee Wee Herman you could get blue eyes too.
Parent	(I told her it would take more than my liking Pee Wee Herman to make my eyes blue. I realised she didn't understand me, so I explained that God gave me this colour and that they couldn't be changed.)
Child	Could you try to like Pee Wee Herman so we could see if your eyes turn blue?
Parent	(I said I would think about it, but if my eyes stayed green it was OK.)

From Callanan, Maureen A. and Oakes, Lisa M. (1992) 'Pre-schoolers' Questions and Parents' Explanations: Causal Thinking in Everyday Activity', *Cognitive Development* 7, 213 -233.

There are a number of important issues in learning science that can be drawn from these examples.

Children's ideas

In example 1 Sophie was initially surprised that her heavy boat floated. She made efforts to balance her boat so it did not sink. In example 2, Nargis talked about the paint melting; in example 4 the child is discussing explanations for eye colour. Research carried out over the last twenty years (see for example SPACE reports (1990; 1991), Driver (1985) or Osborne and Frey-berg (1985)) suggests that children begin to develop ideas from a young age, based on observations and patterns of expectations developed in their interactions with the world around them.

> From the very earliest days of its life, a child develops beliefs about the things that happen in its surroundings. The baby lets go of the rattle and it falls to the ground: it does it again and the pattern repeats itself. It pushes a ball and it goes on rolling across the floor. In this way, sets of expectations are established which enable the child to begin to make predictions. Initially these are isolated and independent of one another. However, as the child grows older, all its experiences of pushing, pulling, lifting, throwing and feeling and seeing things

stimulate the development of more generalised sets of expectations and the ability to make predictions about a wider range of experiences. By the time the child receives formal teaching in science it has already constructed a set of beliefs about a wide range of natural phenomena (Driver, 1983, p2)

Common patterns have been found in these ideas and they often conflict with scientific thinking. This means that learning science may require children not just to take on new knowledge but to change their current thinking. This may involve discussing ideas or testing them out practically as in the above examples. It may require consideration of the words we use and differences between scientific and everyday use of language e.g. differences between melting and dissolving. Some scientific concepts are unlikely to be *discovered* by children, but require specific introduction by the adult, combined with opportunities for children to come to terms with these ideas and apply them in new situations.

Different types of activity in science

The examples above show a variety of ways of doing science. They reflect the importance of play, the key role of practical activity and the value of discussion in exploring and developing ideas. Above all, the examples demonstrate the importance of thinking as well as doing in coming to grips with scientific concepts. These themes are explored in more detail below.

Early years practitioners and many of the resources produced to support early years science emphasise the importance of practical activity. However it is increasingly recognised that there are a number of different purposes for practical activity in science that give different emphases to the areas of development in science outlined at the start of this chapter (see Feasey, 1994). Common categories of activity include:

Basic skills These are activities designed to develop important skills of scientific enquiry such as using a magnifying glass, using measuring equipment or making and using a table to record results. Developing such skills will be important if children are to use them in their future enquiries. For example allowing children to explore how a thermometer responds in different environments, learning to use a measuring spoon or drawing up a chart.

Observation tasks encourage children to observe scientifically, to observe and classify objects and events in different ways, to begin to focus on relevant scientific features and use their current knowledge and understanding. For example children could sort materials in different ways – according to observable characteristics – rough/smooth, hard/soft and increasingly based on their properties – float/sink, waterproof/not waterproof, dissolves/does not dissolve. Observations often lead to questions and investigations. These observations could lead to investigations in the water play area into the best materials for making a boat.

Illustrations In these activities children are given instructions about what to do. The purpose is to illustrate a particular concept or introduce a specific skill. For example in order to introduce the concept of dissolving, educators in one nursery set up a series of jars with water in them and encouraged the children to add one teaspoon of different substances such as sand, flour, salt or sugar in each, stir it and watch what happened. Results were recorded on a simple pictorial chart planned by the staff. This activity was used to intro-duce and reinforce appropriate vocabulary – dissolve, float, sink.

Explorations provide opportunities for children to interact with objects and materials, to see what happens or get a feel for phenomena. In this process ideas may be changed or developed. Explorations can often be extended into more specific investigations. In the examples given, Sophie's exploratory boat making could have been extended into an investigation changing one feature of her boat at a time e.g. height of the sides or the shape/area of the base.

Investigations offer children opportunities to follow up their own ideas and questions, to test out predictions and hypotheses or to solve problems. In doing this children draw on their existing conceptual knowledge and under-standing, on scientific skills and processes and on their understanding of scientific procedures. The crucial difference between investigations and illustrations is that when investigating, the children need to be involved in making decisions about what to measure, what equipment to use or how to carry out the test or record results. For example children could investigate whether warm water is better than cold for washing clothes, whether some marks are more difficult to remove than others or which soap is best.

A final category of activity is ***research***. Some areas of science do not lend themselves readily to practical activity. Children may need to use second hand sources – books, computers, videos and adults as resources for learning. In following up discussions above about babies and inheritance, children could find out about the life cycles of different animals.

All forms of activity have a place in learning science. What is vital is that adults are clear about the purposes of the activities planned and their objec-tives in any particular task. As the examples earlier indicate, play has an important role in learning science and there should be a balance of self-initiated and adult initiated activity.

There are a number of other messages from studies of science activities with young children (Feasey, 1994). First, the development of children's capabilities in science cannot be left entirely to chance. The adult has an important role to play in learning.

> Two opposing ways of approaches to supporting learning have sometimes been presented in the past: leaving children to discover for themselves or telling children the answers. Both are too simplistic. Children need to make sense of scientific ideas and come to grips with scientific procedures for themselves but the adult has a vital role to play in this process. Adults can help children to build confidence in themselves as learners, encouraging them to talk about their ideas, review how they carry out their investigations, debate what their results mean and reflect on what they have learnt. This implies a different balance between practical activity and discussion than has been common in the past, with more time given to discussion and reflection. (Glauert, 1996 p29).

Second, it is important to recognise that concepts and processes are inextricably linked in science learning. In particular, if activities focus on the development of skills or processes in investigations in isolation from the conceptual knowledge and understanding that underpin them, they can become solely mathematics, art or language activities. For example when testing materials or comparing minibeasts, it would be important to draw attention to scientifically relevant features – key properties of materials or important biological characteristics such as number of legs or body parts.

Third, children learn best when activities are set in a meaningful context that relates to their everyday lives and experiences. Starting from children's ideas and questions, using familiar stories, drawing on the experiences of parents and the wider community are several ways of ensuring not only that activities are meaningful but that links are made between science and children's everyday lives.

Finally, practical activity is important, but so too is the talking, thinking and imagining behind it. As the initial examples illustrate, children are engaged in all three from a young age.

The examples given suggest a further important issues in science, the role of language in learning.

The role of language in learning science

Language plays a vital role in learning across the curriculum and science is no exception. Through talk at home and at the clinic, children in the examples given were exploring and developing their ideas about heredity, the needs of young babies and how to keep them healthy and safe. The dialogue between the children and the adult during the washing activities helped to promote the development of scientific processes. The discussion with Sophie about her boats was important to highlight the learning that had taken place. Children need opportunities and encouragement to communicate their ideas to peers and adults, to make their ideas explicit and available for change and development. They need encouragement to articulate questions, explanations, predications and observations. Conversely, activities in science offer rich opportunities for language development in children's first or additional languages. The motivation to communicate is strong when exciting things are happening. New words can be introduced in a practical context. Sorting and classifying activities in particular can help to develop descriptive vocabulary and clarify differences between scientific and everyday use of language. When reporting experiences children can learn to organise their thoughts, sequence events and adapt their contributions to an audience.

Progression in learning

There is much still to be learnt about the development of children's capabilities in science, but there are some features of progression in science that educators can observe. As children gain in experience they may increasingly:

- ask questions and suggest ideas

- offer predictions and explanations based on previous knowledge and experience

- tackle explorations and investigations more systematically, beginning to use measurement and recognise the need for a fair test

- notice patterns in observations

- be able to communicate findings in a variety of ways

- make links between one situation and another and begin to apply ideas in new situations and

- show confidence and independence in their approach to science activities.

Remember that children's responses will depend very much on the context. They will be able to perform much better in situations that are meaningful and familiar.

How can we promote learning in science?

The discussion about children's learning has already begun to suggest a number of ways in which children's learning can be promoted.

Planning a wide range of experiences

Providing a rich environment and identifying opportunities for science learning in everyday provision are key starting points. Some examples are shown on the chart on page 91. These can be extended by introducing particular themes or projects across the science curriculum such as electricity, sound, keeping mini-beasts and making seasonal displays. Alternatively, ideas and experiences introduced through adult initiated activities can be followed up or consolidated by careful planning of everyday provision. For example, a nursery educator who had been discussing hens' eggs and life cycles with groups of children, provided animals for small world play and puzzles of stages in the life cycles of animals which gave her opportunities to discuss and revisit these issues. It is valuable to explore the potential in your local environment – local trees you can observe over time, parks and gardens, interesting buildings, building sites, bridges or stations. What do you pass on your way to the shops or the library that could be the focus of discussion? Find out about the people around you both within the school and outside – staff, parents and governors. They may have skills or experiences they could contribute – perhaps they mend bikes or play a musical instrument.

Having planned a range of experiences, finding ways to promote the development of children's conceptual understanding, their skills, processes and attitudes in science is the next step. This will involve:

Building on children's ideas

Explore ways of finding out about children's ideas through discussion, questioning, looking at their drawings, observing their actions and by encouraging them to make these ideas explicit (see Russell, 1989). Activities can then be planned to extend and challenge children's ideas and encourage them to reflect on what they have learnt. For information about ways of finding out common ideas children have in particular concept area and possible intervention strategies see the SPACE reports.

Encouraging questioning

Questions play an important role in promoting thinking and activity. Harlen (1985) identifies the following categories of question that can be used in encouraging explorations or investigations and in developing questioning skills in both adults and children:

Attention focusing questions – Do you notice..? Have you seen?

Comparison questions – What are the similarities and differences? Which is the longest/strongest etc.?

Action questions – What happens if ....?

Problem solving questions – Can you make a sinker float? Can you make a plant grow sideways?

Developing skills and processes

A range of types of activity is needed to ensure development of the full range of skills and processes. Children's development of skills and processes can be encouraged in a number of ways:

- recording and valuing children's questions – before, during and after activities. Often children's questions emerge while they are engaged in an activity

- planning investigations with the children – How could we find out? Can you think of another way of doing this? What should we use?

- encouraging children's predictions and explanations – What do you think will happen? What would happen if we changed...? Why do you think this is happening?

- spending time talking about findings – What do you notice? Was it what you expected? Can you see a pattern?

- introducing different ways of recording as appropriate – drawings, charts, photographs, making books etc. and involving children in making decisions about the form and content of recording.

Promoting positive attitudes

Educators who provide exciting experiences and demonstrate a positive attitude are establishing an important starting point. Some children will show immediate interest in anything new and be full of questions. Others may need support and time spent exploring with an adult before developing the confidence to try out ideas for themselves. Discussing and modelling safe approaches to work in science and a concern for living things can help promote sensitivity to the living and non-living environment. Creating an atmosphere of trust and fostering debate will help to encourage children to show flexibility and respect for evidence.

Discussing links between science and everyday life

One of the strengths of early years practice is that experiences are set in an everyday context so that these links are potentially easy to make. However children often find it difficult to see connections between one context and another, between what goes on inside the setting and outside in the local environment or between one instance of a phenomenon and another. For example you may have discussed what a plant needs to grow inside – how are these needs met out in the park? You may have tested materials to see which are waterproof. Are the children able to use this in choosing materials for a raincoat or a shopping bag?

General strategies discussed in Chapters 1 and 2 are also important in promoting science learning. These include:

Creating a positive climate for learning

In seeking to ensure that all children are able to take up the opportunities offered, it will be necessary to get to know the children well, to learn about their lives and experiences and to take account of all this in planning. Children will respond better if they can see their lives reflected in the materials and activities organised and if differences in experience or confidence are anticipated, for example with equipment, foods, construction toys or electrical components. Identifying and translating key words you hope to introduce (if appropriate) and reinforcing these through games or displays will be valuable for all children. Finding different ways of introducing activities, for example through talk, display or practical demonstration, will help increase their accessibility.

Valuing all children's contributions, having high expectations of children and trying to avoid preconceptions based on performance in other areas are all conducive to establishing a supportive atmosphere. Science offers a valuable context for children to learn from each other, for exploring similarities and differences between people and for challenging prejudice. Praising children for persevering with difficulties, highlighting what has been learnt from problems experienced, and setting a role model yourself by being open to new ideas can help to create an atmosphere in which children feel able to take risks. And providing regular and constructive feedback to pupils and developing a dialogue about their aspirations and progress can help to build confidence and motivation.

Developing a partnership with parents and carers

Ways in which developing a dialogue with parents and carers can contribute positively to children's learning in science have already been indicated in earlier chapters. This relates to their knowledge of children's experiences and interests, the information they can give about children's science learning out of school and the diverse contributions they may be able to make to your provision for young children. For this dialogue to be effective it needs to include discussion about the aims and purposes of science education with young children and the approaches being adopted in your setting. Having open days or evenings when parents and carers can engage in the kinds of science activities their children are experiencing can be one of the most successful ways of achieving this. The Association for Science Education has developed materials to support home-school links in science (see booklist at the end of this chapter).

Using assessment and evaluation to inform future planning

As suggested in Chapter 2, systematic assessment of children's learning in science and evaluation of both provision and planned activities provide vital feedback to inform future planning. For example, observations of children's interests or questions may suggest how activities could be extended or developed at group or individual levels. When monitoring the patterns of children's activities you may notice that some areas are dominated by particular children, or that play is sustained for short periods only, or there may be very little collaboration or productive talk. This may indicate the need for changes in provision or the need for intervention, supplying further equipment, reorganising the area or suggesting new directions for enquiry.

Acting as a role model

Finally, much of the previous discussion has indicated the importance of the adult as a role model:

- showing interest and enthusiasm
- asking questions, being prepared to try out ideas and make mistakes
- being prepared to change ideas and learning about new areas of science
- demonstrating a concern for the environment and, above all
- valuing and listening carefully to children's ideas.

How can science activities be resourced and organised?

Resources

Many of the resources needed for science are everyday, non-specialist materials. Suggestions for useful science resources both indoors and out are included in the table on page 92. The real challenge is in collecting and organising these materials. Children and adults can be encouraged to participate. Organising resources carefully so they are readily available can help to foster young children's independent explorations and investigations. When using resources it is vital to find out about appropriate safety precautions and to anticipate potential hazards. The Association for Science Education has produced a booklet called *Be Safe* (1990) that outlines the major issues you need to consider in each area of science.

Organisation

How activities are organised will depend on a number of factors – space, the age of the children, the topic being considered, the learning objectives or safety considerations. No one way of working fits all situations. Some activities require close supervision for safety reasons or because the adult wishes to direct children's attention to particular aspects of the task. Other tasks may be left more open and be organised so children can participate when they wish. With older children in a school setting it may be appropriate to plan a day or an afternoon when a number of science activities take place involving the whole class. It will be more practical at other times for only one or two groups to be undertaking science activities. In a single session different forms of organisation may be used at different stages in the activity. When deciding how to organise activities it can help to consider whether your approach will enable children to solve problems and try out their own ideas, whether it will encourage discussion with both adults and children and if it will allow you to listen to children's ideas and build on these in future activities.

Final note

Careful planning, organisation and observation are important in promoting young children's learning in science, but science with young children is tremendous fun. Sharing their interests and trying to keep up with their questions is both rewarding and challenging.

References

Association for Science Education (1990), *Be Safe.* Hatfield: ASE

ASE(1991 and 1992), *School Home Investigations in Primary Science.* Hatfield: ASE

ASE (1992), *Primary Science, A shared experience.* Hatfield: ASE

Driver, R. (1983), *The Pupil as Scientist.* Milton Keynes: Open University Press

Driver, R. *et al* (Eds.) (1985), *Children's Ideas in Science.* Milton Keynes: Open University Press

Feasey, R. (1994), 'Scientific Investigations' in Cherrington, R. (Ed.) *The ASE Primary Teacher's Handbook.* Cheltenham: ASE/Stanley Thornes

Glauert, E. (1996), *Tracking Significant Achievement in Primary Science.* London: Hodder and Stoughton

Harlen. W. (Ed) (1985), *Primary Science, Taking the Plunge.* London: Heinemann Educational

Osborne, R. and Freyber, P. (1985), *Learning in Science.* London: Heinemann

Russell, T. (1989), 'Keeping Track of children's thinking', *Primary Science Review*, National Curriculum Special, Summer 1989, ASE

Sherrington, R. (Ed.)(1993), *ASE Primary Science Teachers' Handbook.* Hatfield: Association for Science Education

Smail, R. (1993), 'Gender Issues in Science Education' in Sherrington, R. (Ed) (1993)

SPACE Research Reports (1990, 1991) for example: *Evaporation and Condensation, Growth, Materials,* Liverpool University Press

GENERAL RESOURCES TO SUPPORT SCIENCE LEARNING

This list suggests some starting points in terms of collecting resources.

INDOORS

exploring materials
water, sand, soil, sawdust, clay, plasticine, salt, flour, paint... liquids – oil, vinegar, liquid soap, glycerine... cooking ingredients...

construction
variety of construction kits, bricks and blocks of different shapes and sizes, pulleys, cogs...

junk
containers of different materials and sizes for example cardboard boxes, plastic pots; variety of papers and fabrics...

moving toys
variety of small wheeled vehicles trains, wind up toys, toys that move in different ways e.g. pushing, pulling, blowing, springs, batteries

living things
keeping plants and animals indoors – mini beasts – snails, caterpillars; plants – seeds, bulbs

collections
materials e.g. metal, wood, plastic etc. and *objects with different properties* e.g. transparent/translucent/opaque; rough/smooth; stretchy or bendy; magnetic; float/sink...
natural materials e.g. fruits and seeds, shells, stones, feathers.
fabrics, threads and strings

equipment for observing closely
magnifying glasses, measuring equipment e.g. scales, spring balances, rules, stopwatches, egg timers, thermometer, measuring jug

sand tray*
colanders, sieves, funnels, sand wheel, forks, trowels, containers of different sizes, moulds...

OUTDOORS

exploring materials
wood, bark, stones, gravel, soil, sand, water – rain, snow, puddles, frost...

construction
crates, tubes, barrels, planks, blocks, pulleys, tyres...

work bench*
tools, sand paper, wood off cuts, cotton reels, nails, screws, washers, bottle tops... objects to explore and take apart e.g. telephones, clocks, radios...

large moving toys
wheelbarrows, bikes, large trucks, scooters..., kites, windmills...

environmental area
tubs and pots, flowers, bushes, trees, logs and stones, pond – both temporary and permanent features.

local environment exploring
opportunities e.g. gardens, parks, local trees, flower beds, buildings, building sites, bridges, ponds, puddles...

climbing equipment
ladders, ropes, swings, climbing frames, see-saw, swings...

water tray•
pump, water wheel, plastic piping, containers, funnels, objects made of different materials, hollow and solid objects.... guttering, boats

Science specific resources:
selection of magnets, batteries, bulbs, bulb holders, buzzers, motors, wire, wire cutters... mirrors, prisms, lenses, colour filters, torches, kaleidoscope, reflectors...

* both indoors and outdoors

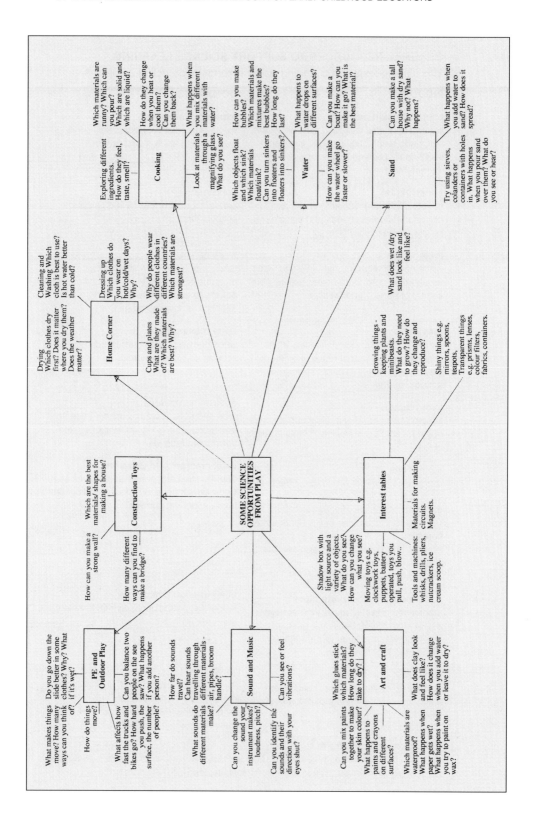

CHAPTER 6

PHYSICAL DEVELOPMENT IN THE EARLY YEARS

Pauline Wetton

Although their chronological age may be much the same when children enter pre-school settings, they will be of different heights, weights and body shapes. Educators should be aware of these differences when planning the physical development area of learning.

From ages 3 to 7, children are entering a crucial life phase. Gallahue (1995) asserts that from 2-7 years of age is the time when the basic motor skills and patterns are developed, so the objective in the early years should be to ensure that all children have the opportunity to develop these skills and patterns. Similarly, Sugden (1990) asserts that children will develop all the funda-mental skills they will ever possess by the time they are seven, so confirming the view that one of the major tasks of childhood is the development and refinement of skilful performance and that it should not be neglected. Theorists agree with the general hypothesis that teaching children to acquire physical skills before their bodies are ready to acquire them is pointless (Malina and Bouchard, 1991, Gallahue, 1995).

Adults concerned with the physical education of children, then, should be-come keen observers of children's movements, to become aware of when children are biologically ready to acquire a motor skill or pattern. If children are to reach their functional potential, educators must recognise the biological, the behavioural and the social domain in which the children are nurtured.

In general, those responsible for the education of children in the early years where the curriculum is based on child development, and those responsible for delivering the National Curriculum at Key Stage 1, which is subject based, know about the physical, social, emotional and intellectual complexities which children present. Although each child is expected to reach similar targets, there are different pathways to be trodden if all children are to reach them. And there are more opportunities to focus on the development of each child's gross motor and fine motor development than when children reach Key Stage 1. So to neglect this area of learning at this life phase is to build up learning difficulties for children which will be much harder to overcome in Key Stage 1, both because the critical developmental stage will have been missed and also because the ratio of educators to children is much smaller.

Knowing that children of this age are usually exclusively motor active, educators should encourage the continuance of 'learning by doing', which children have used since birth, by making full provision for children's developing motor competence. Structured environments, both indoors and outdoors, and a safe and stable atmosphere with commonplace routines ensure that children can feel secure enough to choose to play with the physical objects in the environment. Once children have reached this secure state they can begin to learn higher order movement and physical skills. This is when educators should focus on specific areas of learning and make first assessments. These will probably show that, at this stage in their development, children are capable of performing the following:

Gross motor and locomotor skills
- walk forwards, backwards and sideways (general body management)
- walk on tip-toes (balance)
- show a basic running action (general body management)
- climb up steps or a ladder with one foot leading, maximum step depth 21 cms. (bodily co-ordination)
- pivot around and around on feet (balance and control of the body)
- walk up and down mounds (bodily co-ordination)
- jump up and down on the spot on both feet (strength and bodily co-ordination)
- jump a distance of 36cms (leg strength)
- jump down from one foot to two feet from a height of 45cms. (agility and confidence)

- balance walk along a plank at a height of 18cms. from the ground (balance)

- balance on one (preferred) leg for 4 seconds (balance)

- crawl through a barrel, or tunnel (co-ordination and agility)

Children should also be able to perform the following fine motor skills and eye-hand, eye-foot co-ordination skills, although it must be accepted that some children will not have had the opportunity to handle some of the objects involved because of their cultural nurturing.

Fine motor skills

- place three blocks (2.5cms.- 5cms) on top of each other (eye-hand co-ordination and spatial ability)

- make a straight road with ten building blocks, having been shown an exact replica (eye-hand co-ordination and spatial awareness)

- affix a piece of construction apparatus to a hole in another piece (two handed co-ordination)

- assemble a six piece jigsaw (eye-hand co-ordination and spatial ability)

- paint a person with a head and two other body parts (eye-hand co-ordination and internal representation)

- grip and make marks on a paper with a thick soft pencil (fine motor control)

- copy a circle (fine motor control)

- hammer shapes into a pegboard (manipulative strength and eye-hand co-ordination accuracy)

- make a ball with clay or playdough (one and two handed co-ordination)

- pour water from a jug with a spout into a large container (eye-hand co-ordination and fine motor control)

- thread large beads on to a lace (two handed co-ordination)

Eye-hand and eye-foot co-ordination skills

- catch a large ball thrown by an adult between extended arms (eye-hand co-ordination)

- kick a standing size 4 ball forcibly (eye-foot co-ordination)

- pedal a tricycle along a wide chalked or painted line (eye-leg and eye-hand co-ordination)

- push a large ball away from self across a floor surface towards a target (eye-hand co-ordination)

- pull an empty truck around obstacles 1 metre apart (strength, eye-hand co-ordination, spatial awareness)

All 3 year-old children should be able to perform these tasks when they are observed and assessed during play in the first months in pre-school and they should be targeted for special attention if they cannot accomplish them. The acquisition of fine motor skills is an essential element in all children's educational progress but for some children the acquisition of gross motor and locomotor competencies might be neglected in pre-school situations. It is impossible to overestimate the importance which satisfactory motor development and motor skill acquisition can have on children's ability to learn. Such development should not be left to chance or to the choice of the children themselves. Good muscle control and muscle tone enable children to function more effectively and have fewer motor control problems when they have to sit down and involve themselves in such fine motor tasks as writing and keyboard manipulation.

Research by development psychologists demonstrates that gross motor development precedes fine motor development and that awareness of the trunk and the larger parts of the body and their movement precedes both awareness and control of the small parts of the body. Muscle tone is achieved by regular and constant movement repetitions of the muscles and bone density is maintained by putting stress on the bones during movement. Children's lack of ability in gross motor and locomotor skills can limit their confidence and could lead to social problems in primary school playgrounds. Many children with poor gross motor and co-ordination skills will not have had any experience of playing with other children and not know what to do to gain access to shared play. Others, having learned access strategies, will quickly become outcasts if they do not have the physical competence to take part. Furthermore, targeting and assessment can help to identify children who suffer from a motor deficiency. For example the incidence of dyspraxia, a medical term now given to a condition in children who were formerly classed as 'clumsy', is increasing. This condition is often not diagnosed until they reach primary school. The medical research charity Action Research (Waan and Mon-Williams, 1996) has suggested that as soon as this condition is recognised early specialist treatment should be given.

As far as the curriculum for young children is concerned, the former Schools Curriculum and Assessment Authority (SCAA, 1996) has suggested that the Learning Outcomes for the Physical Development area of learning should focus on five areas:

- developing physical control, mobility, awareness of space and manipulative skills in outdoor and indoor environments

- encouragement to develop positive attitudes to a healthy and active way of life

- children will be shown how to move confidently and imaginatively with increasing control and in co-operation with others

- children will use a range of small and large equipment and balancing and climbing apparatus so that they increase their motor skill ability

- children will have been given opportunities to develop their fine motor skills through handling appropriate tools, objects, construction and malleable materials safely and with increasing control.

These five areas provide a guideline for the structure of a curriculum concerned with the physical development of children in the early years. There is a sixth area in the documentation which needs active consideration, namely the creative area of learning, which includes specific references to dance. Any progressive programme which eventually leads into the subject based Physical Education National Curriculum for Key Stage 1 should have dance as one of its features.

How then should such *areas of learning* be constructed? It is crucial that educators always consider the learners before constructing a curriculum at this first stage. Tanner (1978) has shown that there are wide variations in children's growth patterns and provides evidence which should persuade educators of the importance of a continuous focus on physical education throughout the ages 3-7.

Since children in the early years all have different characters and physiques in pre-school education, they need to be stimulated to develop their personal, social, physical, emotional and intellectual growth at their own rate of learning and this is perhaps the reason why so many pre-schools have chosen to provide a structured play environment based around the SCAA *areas of learning*. There are, however, disadvantages in the structured play approach. As indicated earlier, unless educators are expert at observation and assessment of performance, this system will not work for all children. Researchers (Hutt, 1971, Bruner, 1980, Wetton, 1997) have observed, for example, that some children become 'wanderers' in the free choice of play setting, even when the setting has been splendidly created. Such children seldom focus on any type of play and wander around the environment without purpose.

In addition, some children cannot take part in physical activities because their footwear and clothing restrict their movements, and others are prevented from motor play because of immature motor development i.e. they have poor arm strength or eye-hand co-ordination, so cannot, say, push and pull a truck. Others cannot have a chance to play with trucks, tricycles or balls because they do not have the negotiating skills to ask for a turn. Nonetheless, I have seen many good examples of self-learning in settings where good quality of provision and good goal-setting exists.

Accordingly, educators should adopt a number of different strategies to ensure that all children access the Physical Area of learning and acquire the essential motor skills and patterns in pre-school which will allow them to develop and progress both educationally and socially. So pre-school settings should create:

- structured free play opportunities

- interventionist physical activities for groups of children

- situations where motor skills and patterns are taught

- structured learning activities concerned with the development of games' skills

- structured teacher directed learning activities concerned with gross motor skill learning

- structured teacher directed learning activities concerned with fine motor skill learning

- structured teacher directed activities concerned with creative dance activities.

Planning Environments

Both the indoor and outdoor environments should be set up so that children can practice all their developing motor skills and patterns. It is essential that opportunities exist for fine motor play outdoors and locomotor and gross motor play indoors. But pre-schools provision for physical play and motor learning is uneven. This is especially true of provision for 'learning to move' and 'learning through movement' throughout the different pre-school settings of nursery schools, playgroups and reception classes in infant schools, the latter having least provision of all. Yet many observational studies have high-lighted the need for children to be free to climb, run, chase and become involved in 'rough and tumble' activity.

Pre-schools themselves were once places where children could practise all their emerging physical skills. Sadly, however, more and more are structuring their indoor and outdoor environments in the style of reception classes, thus limiting children's opportunities to develop their gross motor and locomotor skills. Consequently children are much more likely to spend their days being involved in fine motor activities which they are not yet ready to master.

As a result, they may become frustrated and seem naughty. More likely, and almost by way of compensation, the children try to find spaces where they 'are allowed to move' – as in life corners where it is acceptable to crawl like a dog or climb to wash windows or pretend to be a dancing Teletubby. Activity is essential for young learners. When they are variously engaged in activities which give them practice in controlling their body weight and using their bodies in different ways, they learn new concepts and advance their physical and cognitive skills. Remember that at this stage, children are still learning through their body's active involvement with the environment so to expect children to be static for long can only retard their growth.

Planning for physical education

The outdoor environment should be accessible to children for most of the time they are at pre-school age. It should be as natural as possible and should therefore be planned to take account of the following principles and features:

- safety

- stimulation and challenge

- varied surfaces ... hard area, grassed area, slopes, sand, pebbles, cobbles

- variety of shapes ... pathways, stepping stones, barrels, tunnels, mounds, steps, bridges

- variety of large equipment ... climbing frames, boat, tricycles, play house, wheelbarrows, carts and trucks, balance wall, slide, see-saw

- variety of small equipment ... balls, bats, hoops, quoits, sand play tools, large paint brushes (for water painting), soil digging tools

- variety of foliage ... trees, bushes, flowers, grass, hedges, arbors

- spaces to run and jump freely.

If children are not free to choose to play outdoors for most of the day, a minimum requirement for indoors should provide for the Physical Area of Development:

- a wide range of fine motor activities (painting, cutting, drawing, construction, modelling, sawing, hammering, pouring, buttoning, lacing, zipping, threading; brushing, stirring and mixing, picking up and placing; grasping, pulling, pushing; tapping, plucking, shaking and drumming)

- a multi-purpose climbing frame (with a balance bar, steps of varying widths, and slide attachment)

- large toys with wheels

- large building blocks

- space for freedom of movement

- a space and a suitable surface for rough and tumble play

- a space for teacher directed activities.

Once suitable facilities have been established, a programme should be planned which will facilitate the SCAA learning outcomes. Educators should be clear about the nature of the learning goals to be achieved while stimulating the children's movements in the areas of physical provision listed above.

> If children are to receive valuable educative experiences rather than a haphazard set of activities then it is imperative that they are presented with materials and ideas based on systematic planning. This can only occur when the nursery staff are clear in their goals and have sound knowledge of each child's stage of development based upon an individual objective assessment. (Curtis, 1986)

The fine motor activities mentioned above are discussed in relation to the acquisition of skills in other chapters in this book so cannot be considered in depth here. However, many activities connected with gross motor skills, such as throwing and catching balls, lifting and carrying large objects, manipulating vehicles and grasping climbing frames also contribute to the development of the fine muscles of the hands and to eye-hand co-ordination capability. Many of these activities also contribute to the bi-lateral co-ordination of the use of both hands, a system which matures rapidly during the pre-school years.

PE apparatus

A climbing frame is a great asset. Although children usually choose to play on the climbing frame after a concentrated fine motor activity and therefore seem to be 'at play', it is a valuable opportunity for educators to observe children's developing physical abilities. Goals can be defined as follows:

- climbs with one foot leading and heavy reliance on grasping with both hands

- climbs with one foot after the other with heavy reliance on both hands

- can climb up the frame using alternate feet with dexterity and confidence

- can move about the apparatus from one place to another with confidence

- is agile in moving about the climbing frame and transferring body weight

- slides feet first

- slides head first

- can walk along the balance beam one foot after the other

- can walk along the balance beam with confidence, without stepping off

- can walk backwards along the beam

- needs a new challenge ... stand on one leg? stepping stones? narrower surface?

A further provision which educators of pre-school children should explore is that of large wheeled toys. These are conducive to the development of fine motor skills, eye-hand co-ordination skills, eye-foot co-ordination skills, gross motor skills, and spatial awareness, and they can also encourage social skills. Large wheeled toys are excellent for developing all the skills mentioned, especially spatial awareness. Children certainly need physical and manipulative control if they are moving with or on a wheeled toy around other children at play!

Learning goals involving the use of large wheeled toys might be listed as follows:

- can negotiate a turn on a tricycle

- can get on the tricycle and move it with both feet

- can push the toy

- can pull the toy

- is able to move along whilst pedalling the tricycle

- is able to push a wheeled toy in the area without colliding

- s able to pull a wheeled toy in the area without colliding

- can manoeuvre a tricycle when pedalling around obstacles

- is able to push another child in a wheeled toy

- is able to pull a loaded wheeled toy with confidence

- is able to use a tricycle autonomously

- is able to use wheeled toys for many purposes

A fourth area of provision concerns building with large bricks. This provides children with an opportunity to develop several types of bodily co-ordination. In order to pick up a large object and place it in a particular position, there has to be an element of static balance throughout the body. There also is a visual perception element in organising the body and its parts so as to complete a successful transaction. Once the body is balanced and the eyes focused, then the actions can be moulded together to provide a successful sequence i.e. the selection and grasping of the brick in two hands (bi-lateral co-ordination), then the lifting of the brick to the required height (spatial awareness), followed by placement in the chosen area (visual co-ordination).

Here, learning goals might be described as follows:

- picks up the bricks with two hands

- places the bricks on the floor with two hands

- places bricks on the floor to create a pathway or road

- places one brick on top of another

- places several bricks one on top of another

- creates different types of structures

- creates structures to use with other toys.

A fifth area, for 'soft play', might seem to be less important than the other four but observational studies show that some children search for places to 'rough and tumble', particularly after a concentrated and highly focused period with an adult. In addition 'soft play' areas are valuable for children with special needs, especially when they are beginning to try out new motor movements.

The last provision necessary for the physical development of all pre-schoolers is a space in which teachers can direct activities. These activities may be of a special nature or could be concerned with the work of special groups of children. Where indoor space is severely limited, as in a nursery or reception class attached to a primary school, the children should have daily access to the school hall. Directed teaching through small groups is the recommended method for helping children to develop essential competencies. A plan of action might be as follows: Before beginning the activities children should strip down to vest and pants so that those who came to school in restrictive clothing are not disadvantaged. During this changing time educators can help the children to practise valuable fine motor and hand-eye and eye-hand foot co-ordination skills as they unbutton clothes, unfasten buckles, remove shoes and take off sweaters.

Three types of activities can be offered to the children: gymnastics, dance and games activities. Many primary schools have made the correct provision for their younger learners by providing special pre-school equipment. Equipment should be chosen on the basis largely of agreed learning goals, but these items are suggested:

- an Edra system (lengths of balancing equipment, some straight and some curved; stepping skittles)

- a climbing frame with different bar heights and with ladder, plank and pole attachments

- equipment to jump down from (gymnastics stools of different heights and with different coloured tops)

- mats to jump down onto

- a mat for rolling on and rough and tumble activities

Equipment obviously needs to be carefully positioned. All equipment must be checked to see that it is correctly assembled and placed so that there is enough space around it for the children to move without hindrance. Mats should be placed to cushion landings from height.

As with all activities taken in a teacher directed class lesson, there should be adequate warm-up periods before the children start to use the equipment. An action song such as: 'Heads, shoulders, knees and toes' or 'Here we go round the mulberry bush', or 'Simon Says,' might be used both to warm up the children's bodies ready for action and to prepare them to listen to instructions and promote a happy atmosphere. Or the children can warm up different body parts to 'aerobic' type music. Warm-up time is also opportune for children to become involved in practising locomotor skills such as walking, running, galloping, and hopping, skipping and jumping practices around the space. Whichever method teachers use, the aim is to get the children 'huffing and puffing' (and understanding why this is important) and for each child to have moved and stretched each of their body parts (and been encouraged to identify them).

The teacher can then proceed to teach the children about their bodies and the movements they can make, so that the children begin to develop concepts from the experiences which they take part in.

At the same time, the children will become familiar with the language of operations connected with the activities listed in the next paragraph, and will become active participants in their own learning. This can be developed by such activities as standing on tip toes, taking a long stride, balancing on the left and then the right foot, jumping forward from both feet on to both feet, curling up small, stretching up tall, stretching out fingers and toes, pointing to the right, the left, the floor, the door, the ceiling, the teacher, the helpers, and stand still, sit down, jump up, turn around. Some more complicated instructions can follow, designed to help the children to put together several concepts and language structures, including such instructions as: 'look behind you to make sure there is a space; sit down first, then lie down, and wiggle your fingers, arms and legs in the air', and 'stand on two feet and stretch your arms out as far as you can', and ' put both your hands flat on the floor, keep your arms straight and stretch one leg high in the air'. As the children become more cognisant of the language of operations and can identify body parts, this part of the lesson will be a time when the children are taught how to improve significant skills before being asked to try them on the equipment. Initially, the teacher should always spend some time showing the children how to land their bodies from a height and should give the children balancing tasks to practise. Static balances should be accomplished first before challenging the children to control their dynamic balances, which require the maintenance of equilibrium while the body is moving.

After a warm up and a short session concerned with practising and explaining about locomotor and gross and fine motor skills, children should be grouped under the responsibility of each adult. Initially the children should be limited to one or two pieces of equipment so that they have plenty of opportunity to develop some quality movements with the assistance of their adult helper. After a time the children and their adult can move on to another two pieces of equipment. With this management method, the adult can make in-depth observations of each child's movements and assess whether s/he has reached the agreed learning goals. Each session should end with a cool down.

Finally, teachers should resolve how they will record the information about each child's physical development and achievement so that a comprehensive record of achievement can be passed with them to Key Stage 1.

Once children reach statutory schooling age they will be offered the National Curriculum in Physical Education. There are many books concerned with this physical area of learning so what follows are just brief comments on each of the three activity areas.

The staff should structure a programme which builds on the children's achievements in their pre-schools. All the planning should be based on similar principles to those outlined here. Teachers should refer to the book Safe Practice in PE (BAALPE) for expert advice on all safety aspects.

Structure of the lesson: Each lesson should have four sections: a warm-up, a skill learning section, an opportunity for children to apply the skills and a cool down.

Gymnastic activities

The learning goals are to improve static balance; dynamic balance; jumping skills; climbing skills; agility on the climbing frame; agility on the agility tables; and tumbling skills. The National Curriculum in Physical Education documents the targets which children should achieve in gymnastics activities by the time they reach the end of Key Stage 1 and gives information about the end of Key Stage Attainment Target. Gymnastic activities give children an opportunity to develop their gross motor skills and some locomotor skills and if they take part in a well-balanced programme of activities they will have the skill, balance and strength to be able to manage their bodies in most life situations.

Games activities

Games playing gives children a different medium through which to develop their emerging motor skills and in addition they can be used as a vehicle to develop children's social skills and to provide them with an enjoyable activity so that they are encouraged to take part in games as a lifelong activity. Children in the 3-7 age group enjoy playing games with adults and are eventually able to sustain games playing activities either as self-competing activities or with a partner.

Stage One: Games without equipment

Early years games would include 'Ring a Ring a Roses', 'Bobby Bingo', 'The Farmer's in His Den', Statues, 'What time is it Mr Wolf?' Grandmother's footsteps, Jack Frost (an adaptation of musical statues).

At Key Stage 1, children might play Frost and Sun, Crumbs and crusts, Butterfly Touch, Captain's Coming! The Bean Game, The Body Part Game, Colour Corners, Relay teams (maximum of four people).

The skills associated with the above list are:

Running, stopping, turning, pivoting, walking with control, agility in various situations, variation in speed of running, working at different levels. Identification of body parts, listening, spatial awareness, extending language, understanding language, understanding number concepts, understanding forces.

Once the children have become used to playing with others in their class and to the teacher's 'language of operations' they can be introduced to equipment which will help them to develop their motor skills more effectively.

Stage Two: Skills with equipment

Whenever a new piece of equipment is introduced into a lesson the children should have an opportunity to become comfortable with it. They should have plenty of opportunities to play freely with the equipment and be directed into various tasks which will help them to acquire the skills associated with its use. The following list suggests the order in which pieces of equipment could be introduced to children: bean bags, large balls, quoits, small balls, balls of various shapes and sizes, small plastic child-sized hockey sticks, small child-sized bats of various sizes, skipping ropes. Educators should also consider buying various pieces of equipment to help the children to advance their skills, such as: hoops, skittles, markers, baskets and targets which offer opportunities for target practice, negotiating obstacles and the fine tuning of skills. Most schools paint their hard surfaces outdoors with useful lines and patterns which the children can use to refine and advance their motor skills both during lesson time and at playtime.

Games skills can be grouped into four distinct categories: travelling skills, travelling skills with equipment, sending skills and receiving skills. The emphasis in all lessons should be on skill learning – but in a fun setting!

Dance activities

Dance has been shown to be a wonderful medium through which all children, including the disabled, have an opportunity to enjoy the rhythmical activity encapsulated in dance. Dance can be therapeutic, health related and a means by which physical growth and development can be nurtured. Statutory infor-mation is listed in the National Curriculum documentation:

Pupils should be taught :

- to develop control, co-ordination, balance, poise and elevation in the basic actions of travelling, jumping, turning, gesture and stillness

- to perform movements or patterns, including some from existing dance traditions

- to explore moods and feelings and to develop their response to music through dances, by using rhythmic responses and contrasts in speed, shape, direction and level.

(Department for Education and Employment 1995: 3)

The framework, then, is clear and easy to understand and should not create problems for teachers in relation to content. The content of the curriculum for the dance area of activity is sometimes constructed around a cross-curricular programme. Language is always developed during PE lessons but sometimes language development can be targeted in a specific manner. This is parti-cularly useful for children for whom English is an additional language. By targeting language, both action words and word rhythms are created, and finally movement stories can be offered.

Dance educators (Bruce, 1988, Davies, 1995, Wetton, 1995) believe that movement and sound should be considered together for effective dance teaching. The use of voice sounds, body percussion, percussion instruments and all forms of recorded music are thus essential ingredients in dance teaching.

If children receive a broad and balanced curriculum in the Physical Area of learning in pre-school and in the National Curriculum in Physical Education in Key Stage 1, they should grow and develop successfully. They should also acquire knowledge which will inspire them to take part in physical activity as a lifelong pursuit in order to enjoy physical and emotional well-being.

References

BAALPE (1995) *Safe Practice in Physical Education*, Saltwell: Saltwell Education Centre

Bruce, V. (1988) *Movement and Dance in the Primary School*, Milton Keynes: Open University Press

Bruner, J. (1980) *Under Five in Britain*, London: Grant McIntyre

Curtis, A.M. (1986) *A Curriculum for the Pre-school Child: Learning to Learn,* Windsor: NFER Nelson

Davies, M. (1995) *Helping Children to Learn Through a Movement Perspective*, London: Hodder and Stoughton

Department for Education Employment (1995) *Physical Education in the National Curriculum*, London: HMSO

Gallahue, D.L. (1995), *Understanding Motor Development*, 3rd. Edn. Wisconsin: Brown and Benchmark

Hutt, C. (1971) 'Exploration and Play in Young Children' in R.E. Herron and B. Sutton Smith (eds) *Child's Play*, Chichester: Wiley

Malina, R.M. and Bouchard, C. (1993) *Growth, Maturation and Physical Activity*, Champaign, Illinois: Human Kinetics

SCAA, (1996) *Nursery Education: Desirable Outcomes for Children's Learning on Entering Compulsory Education*, SCAA/DfEE

Sugden, D. (1990) 'The Development of Physical Education for All.' *British Journal of Physical Education*, 21 (1): 247-51

Tanner, J.M. (1978) *Education and Physical Growth,* London: Hodder and Stoughton

Waan, J.P. and Mon-Williams, M. (1996) 'Clumsiness in children' on-going research, Horsham: *Action Research*

Wetton, P. (1997) *Physical Education in the Early Years*, London and New York: Routledge

CHAPTER 7

DESIGN, TECHNOLOGY AND THE USE OF COMPUTERS IN THE EARLY YEARS

John Siraj-Blatchford

Craft activities have been considered an important part of early years practice since the beginning of the kindergarten movement, so it is not surprising that a good deal of 'designing and making' continues to take place in most settings. Children model with clay or plasticine, they play with wooden blocks or construction kits, they make things from old boxes, food and drinks containers and other 'recycled' materials. With the support of adults, children make cakes or other food products, and may sometimes help plan and decorate their setting for parties and celebrations. In some early years settings children work with more resistant materials, shaping and joining wood to make things. Comenius, Pestalozzi, Owen and Froebel all extolled the virtues of work of this kind and encouraged educators to provide opportunities for children to make things. Froebel's proposals for the *Volkserziehungsonstalt* at Helba in 1829 recommended that children spend each afternoon in crafts that included making wooden kitchen utensils, weaving, and using pasteboard to make stars, wheels, boxes, napkin rings and lampshades. He suggested that children be encouraged to whittle boats, windmills and waterwheels, and model with clay and flexible wire. For Froebel, education in manual skills served to develop the whole child; it was much more than merely a vocational concern. He believed that craft provided a means of expression and a powerful means to develop habits of success and perseverance.

In recent years a great deal of effort has been put into developing our understanding of design and technology and now we can confidently offer early years educators a degree of guidance that simply was not available ten years ago. This chapter outlines the major principles that determine quality in designing and making, so that early years educators can have the basic information they require to adapt the 'making' opportunities that already form a part of their day to day practices. And to extend this repertoire of designing and making activities the chapter ends with a list of further sources. I also discuss the place of communication and information technology (CIT) in the early years.

Designing, Making and 'Evaluating'

When we 'design and make' things we usually start off with some ideas about what it is that we want to achieve, and in the process of 'making' we evaluate our efforts and modify our designs as we go along. When we prepare food we taste it, and we may add, reduce or change ingredients according to our evaluation of how it is going. Similarly, when we work with textiles, knitting or dressmaking, without rigidly following someone else's pattern or plan, we constantly evaluate our progress and modify our ideas until we are satisfied. Whatever we are making we may elaborate our designs because we have discovered some new material or technique, or purely for aesthetic purposes. When making things from more resistant materials we may choose to select a different material when the one we have been trying proves difficult to shape or fix.

The Assessment and Performance Unit (APU, 1988), who were set the task of developing a model to describe this process, came up with the idea that all designing and making involved a process of interaction between the 'head' and the 'hand': we picture or imagine what can be done in our 'mind's eye', and act accordingly. The process is cyclical because as soon as we do something, the product is evaluated and our evaluations moderate or develop our designs further. The process can therefore be represented as one involving a designing – making – evaluating (dme) cycle (Fig. 1). The cycle is closed because one could, of course, carry on elaborating a design forever. A key task for the early years educator who supports children in their designing and making is therefore to determine the point at which a project should begin, and at what point it should be ended. The first aspect has implications for the kind of support that the child will need; the latter usually determines the quality of the final product.

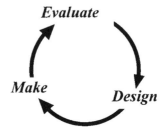

Figure 1

Making

There is no reason to assume that 'designing' must be carried out before handling materials and making things. Edward De Bono defined thinking as 'exploring experience for a purpose', and while such explorations may later become more symbolic than concrete, some form of 'free play' period, where success and failure are irrelevant, may well represent as important an element in the process of design as of making. What is actually needed is a commitment to encouraging children to try out their ideas with materials, to 'prototype'. Children often benefit from working with designs supplied by an adult or that have been agreed collaboratively beforehand. This provides a valuable means of introducing the children to new techniques, mechanisms or structures.

Case Study

A group of children may be introduced to the 'design and making' of sponge cakes by first giving them one of your own reliable recipes (an established design). A Victoria Sandwich recipe would do. That would involve the children in mixing an equal weight of eggs, flour, sugar and margarine before spooning the mixture out into the 'greased' baking tray. The children will have been asked to think first about who they are making the cake for; is it an individual or a group? What are their favourite tastes? Favourite colours etc? Having produced their basic sponge, the children have a wide range of fillings and toppings to choose from in creating their own sponge cake product – designed to satisfy the particular needs they have chosen. The recipe is fairly robust so flavourings and food colourings could also be used (in moderation) before baking.

Children will enjoy making food products, simple pop-up cards, block structures and a wide variety of other products. They can also design and make 'environments' that can be played in and may even be involved in reorganising the home corner for a new theme or topic. Young children find this sort of large scale design and technology work particularly exciting and the collaborative projects that can be developed using commercially available hollow wooden blocks (e.g. Community Playthings) or with structures constructed from recycled materials (e.g. rolled newspaper) are highly appropriate. Very detailed advice on a range of specific activities and techniques available lies beyond this chapter but may be found in Siraj-Blatchford and Macleod-Brudenell (1998).

Collections of recycled and other 'consumable' materials should be kept in the setting and the children given free access to them for exploration as well as more structured designing and making activities. In addition to cardboard boxes and recycled plastic food and drinks containers and fabrics, a number of other useful materials are available from schools suppliers (e.g. TTS – see resources). Wood can be purchased in square section sticks and as doweling, and lollipop sticks, cotton reels, masking tape, tissue paper and art straws are all particularly useful. PVA glue is a must, and also numerous other components for 'joining things up'; e.g. paper clips, paper fasteners, tap washers, string, treasury tags, pipe cleaners, ribbon and wire. Tools should include (good) scissors, paper drills, pinking shears, junior hacksaws, and hand drills.

Children's craft skills, particularly their use of tools, are dependent upon a range of fine motor capabilities. Tools such as scissors, files, hacksaws, hand drills, rulers and compasses all need to be gripped, turned, squeezed, pushed and pulled with varying force and hand-eye co-ordination. The manipulation of components in construction kits demands similar skills. These skills will develop as children are given the experience to practice and this has important implications for girls. Boys have typically benefited from greater experience in making models with construction kits. While some efforts are being made to counter parental tendencies to 'gender' toys by organisations such as the National Toy Council, early years educators also have a role in actively encouraging girls to play with these tools and materials. It is important to recognise that to offer equality of opportunity in terms of equal access and a free choice alone, will be completely inadequate here. When the children go on to school they will find that Design and Technology is a National Curriculum foundation subject and that all will be taught the subject. Brown (1989) has shown that the capability gap between boys and girls can be closed when girls are given encouragement.

Designing

Given the dearth of inservice training for introducing this new subject into schools, it is unsurprising that for many teachers 'designing' has meant little more than children drawing a picture first before embarking on the business of 'making'. As previously suggested, design should be seen as something that is as much a response to making as any prelude. When we design we usually have in mind some existing product design that we are seeking to adapt or modify to our own purposes or resources. We very rarely begin with an entirely new invention and should not expect young children to do so either. I do not know if you can *teach* creativity, but I share with Bernadette Duffy (Chapter 9) the belief that it can be encouraged and is of immense importance. Too often I have seen it actively discouraged by giving children either too much freedom of expression or too little. In the former case the children are unable to realise their design in practice, and do not have the skills, tools or materials to make what it is that they have in mind. In the latter case the educator's expectations may be too narrow and they may be over-directive in requiring children to apply an established design or to use a limited range of materials.

Case Study:

Following a reading and discussion of the story *Mrs Armitage's Bicycle*, an extremely entertaining book that ends with Mrs Armitage falling off, a group of 4 and 5 year-olds were given the challenge of designing a safer bicycle. I had intended that the designs be incorporated in an existing classroom display that featured a child's bicycle. We had been making different 'extras' to fit on the bicycle for the past two weeks. In response to the children's designs I was able to support the children in fixing extra wheels, cushions and 'roll bars' to the bicycle, but one child's design didn't fit in with my expectations at all (Fig. 2). I had expected the children to make things that I could put on the bicycle and at a busy time it would have been very easy to have shown my initial confusion when one of them showed me her efforts. As it was, her lateral thinking was rewarded – I realised that in redesigning the road surface the bicycle was to ride on she had drawn upon her knowledge of the special surfaces placed around climbing bars. The design was therefore presented to the other children with a degree of delight that proved infectious. We managed to find some carpet to put under the bicycle, and quite a number of the children brought a parent into the classroom over the next few weeks specifically for the purpose of showing them the clever idea for making bicycles safer.

If I had expected the children to make their own models of their designs using, for example, recycled materials, they would have found it difficult. A bicycle is a very complicated machine to model. If I had prepared a collection of sticks and margarine tub lids for them to use, failure to use these materials might also have been seen as a problem. In similar circumstances some adults have even been know to tell a child that their design is unsuitable, and even that they should try again!

Young children find it useful to discuss their design ideas at an early stage and research by Constable (1994) has shown that children as young as four may even attempt 3D drawing. But research also suggests that it is only very rarely that children spontaneously attempt a drawing when they are making something. In fact young children often find it difficult to present their design ideas, even in 2D drawings, before they have worked out their solution with the materials themselves. Constable suggests that we might therefore decide not to encourage children to use drawings in their design at all. It seems likely that children's success in this area will actually depend upon the level of detail that is demanded and upon the amount of support provided. Drawings can be used by older children to help them predict the materials and the techniques that they will need and can help them to plan and visualise their design.

Figure 2

While children may not choose to use drawings to elaborate their designs we know that, without support and encouragement, they would not choose to do many of the other things that we value educationally. If we encourage but do not require children to draw their designs, and if we discuss the child's drawings with them during their designing and making work, we can help them to develop their learning awareness and individual capability.

Evaluation

The 'made' environment, along with every technological artefact contained within it, is a cultural product (Pacey, 1983). The development of children's design 'awareness' should therefore be seen as contributing an important part of their general education. Some of the best work currently carried out in the early years has involved the use of collections of domestic or toy product e.g. different forms of: 'baby rattles', 'teddy bears', 'writing tools', 'clothes pegs', 'potato peelers'. Nobel referred to technological artefacts as 'hardened history' and it is worth collecting the stories that go with everyday products. Some valuable 'dictionary of inventions' and other reference texts are now available (e.g. Bunch and Hellemans, 1993 – see resources). When their drawing skills permit, children can usefully be asked to produce 'exploded diagrams' of artefacts and thus focus their attention on detail, on the components and mechanisms that are employed. Even earlier, the evaluation of artefacts from different cultures, for different purposes or for individuals with 'special needs' provides a powerful resource for values education. The undesirable technological side effects of products may be discussed and the 'winners and losers' of implementation identified. Teachers and researchers have found that young children are capable of expressing empathy for others and that role-play activities which involve different points of view can be developed successfully.

'Evaluation' provides a starting point for designing and making when the children are given a structured evaluation activity before selecting their own design. In the example of the sponge cakes cited earlier, a 'tasting' using a range of recipes could have preceded the activity and the children might then have been given a choice of the recipe 'base' for their product design. In learning how to evaluate the things that they make in terms of the needs or opportunities agreed with the adult, or provided by an explicit design brief, children will consider their product's suitability for the purposes initially determined. When it comes to evaluating each others' work it is important to encourage children from the start to define the positive features of each product rather than 'which is best'.

Achieving Quality

The quality of designing and making outcomes depend upon the child's motivation and the level of support provided. Whatever starting point is taken in launching into the design-make-evaluate cycle, stories and poems provide very appropriate contexts for introducing the practical work. Expectations are also really important: if we allow children to leave the classroom with artefacts they have made but feel little pride in, it is unlikely that we will motivate them to improve their work further. Failure can lead to discouragement. When children are motivated to achieve quality they will choose to spend longer selecting suitable materials and developing their ideas before embarking upon the task of making. I have argued here that the level of challenge and degree of support offered by adults needs to be carefully managed.

Information and Communications Technology (ICT)

Computers were first introduced into British primary schools in the early 1980s and by 1990 research showed that half of all junior classrooms were using them. But at that time they were only used in 20% of school infant classes. Many infant teachers felt that computers were unsuitable for infants because they perceived a mismatch between the learning philosophy reflected in much of the infant software available at the time and the most commonly applied and accepted principles of an early years 'developmentally appropriate' curriculum. On the face of it, the use of computers may indeed seem inappropriate. We usually think of individuals using the machines in isolation and given the widespread recognition that the early years is a very important time for social-emotional development, many early years professionals understandably feared that they might inhibit social development.

The evidence is more optimistic however: computers actually seem to act as 'social facilitators' in infant settings. Children prefer to work on computers in groups and while it is not clear whether the computer actually promotes more interaction than other activities there is plenty of evidence to show that the quality of the interaction is high, especially with regard to co-operative behaviour. The main exception to this seems to be related to gender. Boys have tended to monopolise the machines and can become aggressive towards others who want to use it. That said, new information technologies clearly offer great potential in encouraging team work and social development.

Many teachers in the past have also been concerned that some children will be less motivated towards ICT. This seems to have been an extension of the common adult phobia regarding the use of computers and all the evidence suggests that this does not usually apply to children. There do seem to be gender differences here too, but boys and girls are initially equally interested and the only major difference seems to be in software preferences; boys tend to favour arcade type games with targets and scores and girls tend to be more interested in the drill and practice type programs than in open ended ones. This has presented programmers with something of a challenge and we are beginning to see some interesting attempts to break the stereotype.

It has also been suggested that children who are still operating at what Piaget termed the pre-operational level will be unable to benefit from ICT, that as the computer deals almost exclusively with symbols, children will not benefit until they have learnt to classify in at least two dimensions and deal logically with equivalencies and conservation. The sedentary nature of computer use has also been seen as a problem. We all know that infants need exercise and many teachers have been concerned about this. Attention should certainly be paid to ensuring that the equipment is installed on a proper computer desk and that the children sit on chairs that are adjusted correctly. Keyboards/mouse shelves should be slightly lower than the monitor and the screen should be at or only just below eye level.

Access has clearly been a problem that many infant teachers were concerned about. In the early days the standard QWERTY keyboard was clearly unsuitable for infants, and some teachers were particularly unhappy about the upper case letters (some applied sticky labels). A few even reprogrammed their keyboards to provide alphabetical order. The breakthrough came with a device called the concept keyboard which was widely used with BBC computers, and provided a means of selecting pictures and/or whole words instead of individual characters. To a large extent this function is now provided by the use of a mouse pointer or touch sensitive screen and there can be little doubt that these options will be extended in a variety of ways using new input/output technologies. One inexpensive alternative to the mouse that should be considered for very young children is the trackball. This sits in a static base and infants find it easier to control. The standard 'mouse', though, does provide a very effective pointer that most children are very quickly able to use with confidence. The need for adult supervision depends mostly upon the software involved. A program such as Kid Desk is well worth considering, as it provides the means of controlling access but will give the child greater independence in their use of the machine. You will find that young children can quickly learn to turn the machine on and off, replace discs properly and follow instructions from picture menus.

Generally, then, the initial concerns about ICT have proved largely unfounded. Some were based on a misapplications of Piagetian 'stages of development' and it is now widely recognised that children's thinking is not as limited as was once assumed. We also now have research evidence of the benefits of computers to infants. There is evidence that information technology can enhance learning and may be especially useful in providing a means by which children who are not very motivated by the academic curriculum may be drawn in. We also know that a computer can also be helpful with children who suffer poor attention/concentration spans.

While the perceived problems with computer hardware may have been largely unfounded, the criticism regarding the value of the more 'dedicated' early educational programmes have proved much more difficult to deal with. The problem has been that a great deal of the software available is based upon behaviourist learning principles – principles often explicitly rejected and replaced by more progressive early years practices. A few concrete examples illustrate some of the problems with much of the software that is currently available:

'Stickybear's Reading Room' is a fairly sophisticated example of the sort of number/letter/phonic 'drill and practice' programmes available in British infant settings. Others include 'Animated Alphabet and Numbers', 'The Oxford Reading Tree', 'Letterland'. 'Stickybear's Reading Room' runs on a Macintosh computer and includes a routine called 'Word Bop' which children could probably use without supervision. It involves word recognition and this may be developed in some children, but word recognition is not required for the arcade game so many children are likely to play with it repetitively. Another routine in the 'Reading Room' is 'Word Match', designed to build vocabulary for early readers (the blurb claims that word recognition by phonic analysis is enhanced by the program...).

'Word find' is a close procedure that builds literal comprehension using a play/test mode. Then there is 'Sentence builder' which allows children to create their own sentences – the computer animates them, prompts them to read it and then plays their recording back. The program has 86 nouns and 48 verb phrases but, interestingly, while the software refers to an astronaut, an acrobat, clown, diver and 29 animals there are no children included. The people that the child might identify with are therefore all adult and they are also stereotypically male. And this is compounded by the artefacts – bulldozers, garages, motorcycles, submarines and rockets. There are no prams, shopping trolleys, department stores or kitchens. The program thus has an inbuilt bias towards boys. The verb phrases are also restricted: it is possible for the astronaut to move in a wide variety of ways e.g. fly, jump, even skip – but he cannot sit, talk, laugh, cry or hug anyone.

Another example of a drill and practice programme of this sort, also available for the Macintosh, is 'Millie's Math House'. This includes 'Number Machine' and 'Bing/bong' which encourages children to complete patterns the program makers claim will: 'empower children to recognise other patterns in music, mathematics, art, and science and to make better sense of the world'. This program typifies the behaviourist teaching approach (learning theories based on behaviour modification) that is inherent in many of the programs of this genre. If the child gets a right answer they are rewarded by some amusing action sequence and/or tune. If children make a mistake the options are gradually reduced until they are forced to make the 'correct' response.

So, is any kind of computer or software better than none?

Children who spend too much of their time sitting in front of a computer screen are undoubtedly missing out on a range of other important activities and experiences. But as part of a balanced curriculum computers offer much value. The biggest problem concerns the mismatch with learning philosophy, as we have seen. Boys like arcade games but are they educationally suitable? Poor software has been shown to demotivate children. We certainly need to consider young children's preferences but we also need to consider the child's personal and social education and the 'hidden curriculum'. The most significant argument that has been consistently put forward has been that computers cannot provide a free-flow play learning environment. Computers require turn-taking and other interactive skills but the crucial question has been: who has control – the child or the computer program? This is an area that deserves greater attention and one that offers a good deal of developmental promise.

Content free software opens up the possibility of developing a more integrated approach to the use of ICT in the early years. Framework, generic or content free computer programmes still offer much more scope for early years education than the more sophisticated learning programmes. ICT and design and technology education have a great deal to offer the early years, but, as with most things, what we (and our pupils) get out of these activities depends to a large extent upon the investment in terms of time and energy that we are willing to put in, in preparation. It is certainly worth it.

Recommended Published Resources

Bunch, B., and Hellemans, A. (1993) *The Timetables of Technology*. London: Simon and Schuster

Jones, A. (1988) *Things for Children to Make and Do*. London: Souvenir Press

Kimbell, R. (1996) *The Journal of Design and Technology Education: The DATA Journal*

Siraj-Blatchford, J. (1997) *Learning Technology, Science and Social Justice: an integrated approach for 3-13 year-olds*. Nottingham: Education Now

Siraj-Blatchford, J. and Macleod-Brudenell, I. (1998) *Supporting Design, Technology and Science in the Early Years*. Buckingham: Open University Press

Catalogues are available from:

Rickett Educational Media (REM) Great Western House, Langport, Somerset, TA10 9YU. Tel 01458-253636 Fax 01458-253646

SEMERC, 1, Broadbent Road, Watersheddings, Oldham, OL1 4LB Tel 0161-6274469 Fax 0161-6272381

Technology Teaching Systems (TTS), Monk Road, Alfreton, Derbyshire, DE55 7RL Tel 0800 318686 Fax 0800 137525

If you have access to the internet the following addresses are worth exploring for software reviews:

http://www.superkids.com

http://www.kidsdomain.com

http://www.logo.com

References

Brown, C. (1989) 'Girls, Boys and Technology; getting to the roots of the problem: a study of differential achievement in the early years', *School Science Review*, Vol. 71 (255), p 138-142, December

Constable, H, 'A Study of aspects of design and technology capability at Key Stage 1 and 2', in Smith, J. (Ed.) *IDATER 94*, Loughborough University of Technology

Pacey, A. (1983) *The Culture of Technology*, The MIT Press, Cambridge Mass.

Siraj-Blatchford, J. and Macleod-Brudenell, I. (1998) *Supporting Design, Technology and Science in the Early Years*, Open University Press

CHAPTER 8

HUMANITIES – DEVELOPING A SENSE OF PLACE AND TIME IN THE EARLY YEARS

Caroline Heal and John Cook

In this chapter we explore the earliest learning-about-the-world that young children do, concentrating on the dimensions of 'time' and 'space', because how children develop understandings about these aspects of the world will provide the basis for their school learning of 'history' and 'geography'. Adults trying to help children in all their learning need to build gradually on what they already know. Understanding children's extraordinary capacity for learning means thinking back to the processes of their learning in the earliest stages.

Building on children's earliest experiences

At birth infants have no experience of the world outside the womb. Within a few weeks they communicate quite clearly that they are sorting their experiences and becoming familiar with aspects of the world around them. They are making sense of their sensory experiences and building up associations on the basis of the experience they are acquiring. A tiny baby recognising and responding to the face of a familiar carer is showing us something about the deep significance of 'time' and 'space' in developing their understanding of the world. Recognition of that familiar face can only take place because the face has been seen before and been remembered; thus the baby is making a connection between the past and the present through memory – the beginning of a personal history. In the same way the face is only familiar because of the way it looks – the 'map' of it – and this is the start of a personal geography. These personal histories and geographies build up very quickly indeed.

This rapid learning is fed by all the experiences of early childhood. The substance of these experiences will vary from child to child but all children share the process. One of the challenges of early years education is to appreciate this growth of knowledge and understanding within the home and neighbourhood environment and to support and extend it. So a key aspect of good early years practice is providing children with experiences that relate to and build on what they already know. Using and building upon their experiences of spaces and places, the memories they have and the stories they hear and can tell about the past is essential.

Let's think first about the experience of 'place'. All children are aware of places and have experience of exploring them from when they start to move around. They learn that the rooms in which they live have different purposes and different potential for play; they visit other homes, nearby playgrounds or open spaces. There are outings to the shops, to supermarkets, and places for special visits – a McDonalds, the wider family, the doctor. The adults around them point out things of interest, introduce new words and the vocabulary of street, shop, town or countryside begins to develop. Some journeys are becoming more familiar every time they make them and the ones they take regularly are becoming very well known indeed.

Further afield, holidays allow young travellers to experience new and contrasting places. There is growing evidence to suggest that children are more 'travelled' than their counterparts of twenty or thirty years ago, and yet as they get older and ready for independent travel, the range of places they are allowed to go on their own may be becoming more restricted as parental concerns about safety increase (Hillman, 1993). It may be that children are becoming more aware of the wider world at the expense of an intimate knowledge of their local area. There may be cultural and gender differences here: boys are often given more freedom than girls to explore their surroundings without supervision. These differences can be taken into account in planning experiences for children.

One obvious difference between the awareness of 'place' and the awareness of 'time past' is that places exist in the here-and-now and can be experienced, but the past has in some sense 'gone' and has to be accessed in some other way. This is one of the apparent features of history that had led some people to think that it is too abstract for very young children. However if we think about how a sense of time past builds up from the earliest stages, it is clear that young children have powerful ways in. First and foremost the children's own memory provides a personal past. They remember their own past experiences ... of family members, of places, of meal times, of previous occasions when things happened and they did things. Much family talk of an everyday sort refers to these past experiences. Children may not have much sense initially of 'when?' or 'how long ago?' but they do understand 'before now'.

The other important way that a sense of the past is developed is through stories, both the stories children tell back to themselves about their experiences: 'Yesterday I fell over and hurt my knee', and the stories that other people tell. Adults telling and retelling stories about the children's experiences in the past or their own, however fragmentary, are contributing to their sense of who they are and where they have come from. And then there are all the other stories, the reminiscences, the narratives rooted in community life, the stories told by friends and family, the folk tales, myths and legends, and the stories on television and in books.

The development of knowledge and skills – what research into the processes of children's learning tells us

As children develop a sense of their place in the world – a mental map of where they are in space and time and an ability to imagine and think about the world – this profoundly influences their sense of personal identity. Their mental maps become more sophisticated as experience grows.

Greater familiarity with a wider range of different environments accelerates the process. We have evidence that concepts of place and space develop early. Cornell and Heth (1983) noted the ease with which young children could retrace a route after walking it only once. Atkins (1981) taught four year-old children about maps, globes and compass directions and compared their knowledge and understanding with a group who had had no teaching. When she tested the children she found that the group she had taught did better in the tests both immediately after the teaching and a year later. Wiegand (1993) suggests that geographical skills emerge at a very early age, pointing out that young children often try to draw maps, plans or pictures of places before they read or write. Children's abilities to read and use a simple plan of a room was a focus for research by Blades and Spencer (1986). Beginning with a scale model of a familiar room, children aged 4-6 were asked to locate treasure 'hidden' in the actual room and then find their own position in the room using the model. Most of the children could do this. They could walk simple routes in the nursery playground by following routes shown on a 1:50 scale plan. They could find their way through a simple maze using a plan showing its layout. Further investigation by the same researchers showed that children aged 4-6 could recognise especially designed symbols on a map, with roads, rivers and parks easily identified by most children. Somerville and Bryant

(1985) have shown that young children (aged 4-6) can use co-ordinates in simple tasks.

It would appear then that pre-school and children commencing Key Stage 1 can show considerable spatial understanding. They demonstrate remarkable confidence when aspects of mapwork are introduced in the context of known or 'pretend' settings. The nursery classroom and outdoor environment offer many opportunities to extend these areas of learning.

Although understanding the conventions of the measurement of time does not develop quickly, young children clearly show that they can understand the nature of a chronological sequence of events and understand that people have reasons for the things they do and that actions have particular consequences. All these elements are crucial to historical understanding. Cooper (1995) summarises research into the growth of children's ideas about time and gives examples from her work with teachers, often stimulated by discussing story books with children, that shows how keenly they search for meaning in the stories they encounter. They make comparisons and notice similarities and differences. If opportunities to use these skills are provided in familiar contexts then children show that they can do a great deal.

Another significant aspect of learning about the past, for children as well as adults, is connected to the way the past is, by definition, no longer available to be studied directly. We cannot turn back the clock in order to see what happened, and even if we could, we certainly would not be able to 'see' explanations of why they happened! Our knowledge and understanding of the past is always an interpretation according to what has been left behind. And what is left behind can take many forms – stories, eye-witness accounts, diaries and letters, memories recounted or written down, buildings and monuments, sound recordings, objects, photographs, paintings and other images of all kinds. All can provide opportunities to speculate about the past. And the tantalising thing about these 'leftovers' from the past is that they do not in themselves tell us the story; they have to be re-interpreted. Consequently, versions of the past are reconstructions – interpretations that people have made that can be remade in the light of new or different evidence or a different point of view. All this makes finding out about and understanding the past a challenging piece of detective work which children can be involved in, in the same way as, and alongside, adults.

Clearly then, an important part of learning about places or about past times is developing special skills of enquiry. Many enquiry skills are common across the curriculum: observation, for instance, and questioning, hypothesising and devising ways of finding out. Central to history is the skill of evaluating evidence, asking and trying to answer the question 'how do we know?'. And in geography, making, using and interpreting maps are central skills – the skills of graphicacy.

The greater challenge of the wider world, the more distant past and the growth of common misconceptions

Children also show how their ideas about the more distant past and the wider world build up – their growing historical and global awareness. A number of research studies have explored the images young children have of the world and found that they are confident to represent their maps of the world in their drawings. Early maps tend to be pictorial, showing houses and trees, but many children also show awareness of 'countries' and the conventions of representing land masses and seas. Wiegand (1991) found that by age 7 and 8 children are generally able to name five or six countries, usually the larger land masses such as America, India, China and Australia. They may sometimes name fantasy lands such as Disneyland or Legoland but their awareness of other places grows steadily.

Children can discuss what is 'old' and what is 'new' and talk about the basis for their judgements. There is evidence that young children are able to put items or events or periods in history in sequence well before they make reliable judgements about date or duration (West, 1981). They can discuss the important difference between real and pretend. Much of the research into children's understanding of television suggests that they learn very early to recognise fiction and to make quite sophisticated judgements about what might be real and what just pretend.

Children are also aware of the nature and quality of environments. Joy Palmer (1993) has identified what she calls their 'emergent environmentalism'. She used photographs of different environments to encourage nursery children to talk and found that they were aware of issues such as the destruction of the rainforest, global warming and the problems of waste. Clearly this growing knowledge of the wider world is associated with experience of travel, television and film, books and picture images.

In this wider context, research points to the beginnings of biased, stereotypical knowledge developing, certainly by the middle primary years (Storm, 1984; Stillwell and Spencer, 1974). Aboud (1988) suggests that children as young as 4 express negative responses to other ethnic groups. Helping children to develop a more informed understanding of other peoples, past and present, and must inform our teaching in these curriculum areas. This connects directly to our wider responsibilities for education for citizenship and membership of an interdependent global community.

Thus we should not underestimate the significance of young children's observations and awareness of the wider world and the distant past. An early years curriculum needs to take account of all these issues and build upon and promote a variety of rich experiences to develop the children's ideas and thinking further.

Shaping the curriculum – some issues for planning

A curriculum for the early years has always emphasised first hand experiences which give children time and space and play opportunities to explore and develop their ideas of the world and to make sense of them. The children are beginning to decentre, to appreciate that there are other points of view, and are moving towards symbolic interpretation and representation. In planning a curriculum for the early years, teachers have seen the growth of children's time and place based knowledge and skills as located within the 'human and social' area of learning. However, this has always encompassed a broad spectrum of learning, with many links to other areas (language, literacy, and personal and social education in particular). Within the definition 'human and social', we could also include learning about how we live and the world of work, about relationships with others and with the environment, about events and actions in the past and their relationship to the present and the future, and about all aspects of physical and human conditions.

The Desirable Outcomes for Children's Learning (SCAA, 1996) has identified the goals for learning for children by the time they reach compulsory education in the term after their fifth birthday. The outcomes for the key area 'knowledge and understanding of the world' focus on children's developing knowledge and understanding of their environment, other people and features of the natural and made world. They provide a foundation for historical, geographical, scientific and technological learning. This is emphasised in the matrix produced by SCAA which shows how the desirable outcomes provide a foundation for Key Stage 1 of the National Curriculum.

Responding sensitively to initiatives from children

So what are the opportunities that we need to take up when we work with young children to develop their learning in these areas of the curriculum?

Scenario: The teacher noticed that a child was particularly intrigued by a picture of a castle in a storybook, so she collected together several other pictures of castles. The castles were of different types but they also appeared in different picture contexts: one in a traditional fairy story, another in a comic fantasy where the characters were animals, another in an information

Area of Learning	Desirable Outcomes on entry to compulsory schooling	National Curriculum level 1 description
Knowledge and understanding of the world.	Children talk about where they live, their environment, their families and past and present events in their own lives. They show an awareness of the purposes of some features of the area in which they live.	Pupils recognise and make observations about physical and human features. They express their views on features of the environment of a locality they find attractive or unattractive. (Geography).

Pupils recognise distinctions between past and present in their own and other people's lives. They know and recount episodes from stories about the past. (History). |

book about castles with cut-away drawings to show general aspects of castle architecture, and one was a contemporary photograph of a castle in a surrounding landscape taken from the air. Conversation with the child and other children who became interested helped them to speculate about how castles are different from other buildings, why they were built, what sort of people lived in them and how they lived. In addition the children were able to talk about the different ways that the castles were shown in the pictures and why. The teacher encouraged the children to draw and build castles of their own.

Providing opportunities for role-play

Scenario: All the classes in an infant school were learning about life in Britain in Victorian times. All the children had had the opportunity to see and handle many different domestic items from the period, borrowed from the local education authority loan collection and from the families of the children and their teachers. The children in one class had visited the home of a parent and watched a coal fire being lit in an original Victorian fireplace. In their classroom they turned the role-play area into a Victorian parlour with a 'period' fireplace complete with hand-painted 'tiles', coal scuttle, fire irons and mantlepiece ornaments. The props were a mixture of authentic artefacts and 'replicas' made by the children, who were encouraged to consult picture sources to help them to make their replicas look as real as possible. Through the work the children became knowledgeable about the processes involved in maintaining a coal fire, some of the 'work' in a middle-class Victorian house-hold and about who might be likely to do it.

Partnership with parents and carers

Scenario: A first school held an open afternoon for parents to introduce the topic for the term: 'Journeys'. The displays included maps of Britain and the world, showing the journeys adults in the school had made to come to live in the area. The curriculum plan, in the form of a topic flow-chart, was on display for parents and carers to see and examples of work done by the children on important journeys in their lives were shown on time lines. Images of places and of different ways of travelling now and in the past and in different places in the world, stimulated much interested talk and reminiscence about journeys made. A display of story books about journeys and travel included examples of stories that parents had contributed to.

The bilingual captions read:

This is a story which parents have translated. Can you help us to translate some other stories?... This is a story written by a mum for her child. Would you like to write a story for your child? ... This is a picture story about a child's first journey. Would you like to put words to the pictures? Source: S. Hazareesingh: *Speaking about the past, Oral history for 5-7 year-olds* (see Recommended Reading p.133).

Objects associated with home and other places were displayed, along with drawings, letters and cards sent are received by children to friends and family in other places, especially to celebrate the special occasions of Eid, Divali, Christmas, Hannukah and Chinese New Year.

The experience of the open day encouraged parents and carers to contribute in many ways as the work continued. They brought in objects and photos, shared their memories and made tape-recordings and books.

Topic planning

Scenario: As part of their topic 'Ourselves' children in the nursery class talked about their journey to school: who brought them, how they got there, what they passed by on the way. A large scale oblique aerial photograph generated much interest and the children began to point out what they could see: the nearby park, the railway track and station, houses and flats, cars in the streets. They looked down from above at their small world town created on the play mat. Some of the children retraced their journey to school with one of the support staff taking photographs along the way. Back at school

Figure 1: Lorella's map

these were used to relive the journey, trying to organise and sequence the photographs, and even drawing a simple map representation of the route (Figure 1, Lorella's map, age 4 years 8 months). The graphicacy theme was continued by the nursery teacher, who drew a simple plan of a small area of the nursery environment. She introduced the plan to pairs of children and invited them to find the small teddy who was hiding at the point marked 'X'. She recorded the children's responses. Her observation notes included:

> James and Jacob – *'understood directions, found teddy (visible) almost immediately, and the second and third time. James was the leader and used the plan very effectively.'*

> Jaxen and Nicole – *'J and N quickly located the correct area. They were not very good at making a thorough search of the sand tray area. Neither child thought of looking underneath the sand tray and eventually I had to hint about looking higher and lower.'*

> Jensen and Mark – *'I explained the plan at length and they seemed to understand what everything represented but when they set off to look for it they just rushed everywhere looking up and down and from left to right. ... I went through the plan with them again and we pinpointed it to the music table ... they rushed over and immediately found the treasure under the tambourine'.*

Planning provision and activities

If we take the learning outcome from the guidelines for Desirable Outcomes 'Children talk about where they live, their environment, their families and past and present events in their own lives', we can show how a variety of activities can be set up to which children can respond in different ways. It is important that a statement of this kind is not regarded as a superficial short term goal but as an area of learning where the children can explore and develop a range of understanding, skills and abilities over time. It could be summarised as follows:

Children talk about where they live, their environment, their families and past and present events in their own lives

What to provide	Development of language/ Things to say
Carefully planned classroom layout with clearly labelled areas and access to high quality resources.	Look and talk about what is in our classroom and our school and how it is arranged. Can you find what you need? Involve children in decisions about where and how to keep things.
Relevant role-play area(s) with a historical or geographical theme, for instance: museum, baby clinic, travel agent, castle, map-making workshop.	Sensitive adult participation in the play will extend it. Is there someone who can show me round the museum? What can babies do, what do they need? Where should I go on my holiday? What will I need to do to get ready?
Support for role-play – props, equipment dressing-up clothes.	
Play mats, small world toys.	Encourage the use of positional language: What is next to the tower? Which way should we go to the hospital?
Construction play – hard and soft landscaping materials – bricks and blocks, sand and water.	How will the train get across the river? Can you change what you have made? Can you make a plan of your model?
Pictures, photographs, simple plans, globe, models.	What can you see? What is happening here? What do you think these people are doing? Why? What do you think they are feeling/thinking about? What are they going to do next?
A range of objects to look at and touch that have historical or geographical significance.	What is this made of? Is it old or new? Who do you think owned it? What do you think it was used for?
A range of books, fiction and non-fiction, chosen for their historical and geographical themes. Include books made by and for the children, especially about themselves, their families and their experiences.	Talk about the stories, look at the pictures. Do you remember when this picture was taken?
Focus on the sequencing of events and on the reasons why things happen. Encourage the children to think about human motivation and decision-making.	What will happen next ? Why did she do that? Encourage provisional language – 'maybe', 'perhaps'.

Involving the community

Be aware of all the adults in the school community.
Do they have interesting stories to tell about the places they come from, journeys they have made, memories they have and things they could show?

Planned activities

Focus on the classroom layout indoors and outdoors; where things go, labelling, relationship to a simple plan of the parts of the area.

Treasure hunt using simple plans.

Drawing in plan form, looking down, around objects, for others to identify.

Developing the role-play area, thinking about what it needs, making props for it. Include a focus on the local area – the corner shop.

Develop and use time lines of all kinds: time lines that reflect the children's lives and those of their families.

Walking around the school talking about the use of space, who works in the building, who visits, what else our building might need, relationship to a simple plan. How has our school changed?

Planned talk about where they live, journeys to school, using parents to help in photographing parts of the journey, drawing picture maps.

Similar focus upon our house, who lives there, photographs, drawings.

Play with small world toys to allow reconstruction of real journeys and imaginary ones.

Go for walks in the local area, the shops, the park, take photographs, draw maps, pictures of where we went, book making.

Encourage the children to ask questions, to listen carefully, and sometimes to record what they found out.

How was it the same when you were little, and how was it different?

What jobs do people do?

Involve the children in following and giving directions:
How do I get to ...?
Which is nearer ...?
Which is further away ...?
Can you follow this plan ...?

Can you make a puzzle for your friend?

Talk about the environment. Who works in the shop? Who uses it? Has the building always been a shop? How has it changed?

Can you put these in order? What happened first? Which is the oldest/ youngest?

Alongside their parents talk about their home environment, their journey to school.
What do you pass by on the way? Do you see a ... ?
Do you remember?

In our house what is upstairs? downstairs?
Are the shops closer than the school?
Develop vocabulary, lists of new words through visits, recall through photos taken, making books, games to play.
Encourage children to express their opinions.
Is our school clean? tidy?
I like living here because ...

Ways of recording by the children.
Maps, pictures, models, plans, drawings, tape recordings, sequencing photographs, pictures of journeys.

So we know what the outcomes should be for our humanities teaching with younger children and we can see a variety of creative and interesting ways in which they can be achieved. OFSTED guidance (1996) is clear that teachers should provide a range of opportunities for young children to explore the outside environment and the community and allow them to ask questions and explore the world around them. It highlights linking the experiences back in the classroom through talking, drawing, painting or modelling what the children have seen using a range of materials. Planning for progression and continuity is important and besides overall topic headings and brainstorming of ideas needs to address:

- the levels of planning, long, medium and short term

- linkages with other areas of learning

- progression towards the next stages: history or geography led units in the reception class and into Key Stage 1

- assessment opportunities and building upon what we know of the children's skills, knowledge and experience of time and place

- the use of other adults in the nursery setting, groupings of pupils and differentiation

- whether to include aspects beyond the desirable outcomes such as building upon the children's obvious knowledge of the wider world and the distant past.

There is clearly a greater emphasis on the consistency of practice, though the desirable outcomes only so far in terms of what we know young children can do in this area of learning.

Recommended reading

Claire, H. (1996) *Reclaiming our Pasts, Equality and Diversity in the Primary History Curriculum*, Stoke-on-Trent: Trentham Books

Cooper, H. (1995) *History in the Early Years*, London: Routledge

Durbin, G., Morris, S. and Wilkinson, S. (1990) *A Teacher's Guide to Learning from Objects*, London: English Heritage

Hazareesingh, S. (1994) *Speaking about the past, Oral history for 5-7 year-olds*, Stoke-on-Trent: Trentham Books

Martin, F. (1996) *Teaching Early Years Geography*, Cambridge: Chris Kington Publishing

Milner, A. (1994) *Geography Starts Here! Practical approaches with nursery and reception children*, The Geographical Association

Palmer, J. (1994) *Geography in the Early Years*, London: Routledge

Wood, L. and Holden, C. (1995) *Teaching Early Years History*, Cambridge: Chris Kington Publishing

Sources of ideas and materials and places to visit

The local community

The families of the children and other people in the local community are the most valuable resource. The better your communication with families and the more sympathetic your links with the wider community, the more opportunities will be available. Letting families and friends know what opportunities you want to create for the children gives them a chance to contribute ideas, expertise, experiences and resources. Impressive collections of resource material have been built up through relationships with parents and carers.

Think about the organisation of resources so that they are valued, properly looked after and accessible. Keep a record of contacts.

The local area

Get to know your local area. Local maps, planning documents, local history materials available from public libraries and talking to local people will help you to develop knowledge of the area, especially if you do not live locally yourself. Collect resources, take photographs. Let the children know what you are doing, model the attitudes of interest and curiosity and the processes of research for the children and involve the children in it whenever possible.

Local history collections in libraries may have a librarian who is expert and can help you. Some Local Education Authorities have built up collections of historical and other artefacts for loan to schools.

Museums and galleries

Look out for the smaller and local museums and galleries, as well as the major collections. Many museums and galleries are expanding their education function and also producing materials to be used in the classroom. They are becoming much more aware of the needs of younger children. You can speed up this process by making contact with Education Officers and asking about support for teachers of the younger children.

Private individuals are collectors too and are often delighted to bring a treasured collection in to show a group of children. Try local hobby groups – for instance someone from the local archeological society might bring tools and photographs from a dig to show; pot-holers or rock climbers have special equipment and exciting experiences to share.

The Geographical Association

160 Solly Street, Sheffield

S1 4BF

Telephone +44 (0) 114 296 0088

Fax +44 (0) 114 296 7176

The Geographical Association is the professional association for teachers of geography. It offers a range of publications updated all the time, publishes journals including *Primary Geography* and holds conferences.

The Historical Association

59A Kennington Park Road, London

SE11 4JH

Telephone 0171 735 3901

Fax 0171 582 4989

The Historical Association is the professional association for teachers of history. It holds conferences and offers an expanding range of publications and publishes journals including *Primary History.*

The Development Agencies

Many of the agencies working in the area of 'development' see increasing awareness of development issues through education as an important part of their work and are putting energy and expertise into producing materials for teachers. Organisations such as Oxfam, Save the Children, Cafod, Christian Aid make available an increasing range of materials of very high quality. They produce materials that help to develop awareness of a range of places and on human relationships and the importance of co-operation and interdependence in any setting. Many have Education Officers with expertise in primary education who will advise or visit.

There is also a national network of Development Education Centres which can be used as sources of materials and advice. The Development Education Association can supply details:

DEA

29-31 Cowper Street, London

EC2A 4AP

Telephone 0171 490 8108

Fax 0171 490 8123

References

Aboud, F. (1988) *Children and Prejudice*, Oxford: Blackwell

Atkins, C. (1981) 'Introducing basic map and globe concepts to young children' *Journal of Geography* 80, 228-233

Blades, M. and Spencer, C. (1986) 'Map use in the environment and educating children to use maps' *Environmental Education and Information*, 5, 4, 187-204

Cooper, H. (1995) *History in the Early Years*, London: Routledge

Cornell, E. and Heth, C. (1983) 'Spatial cognition: gathering strategies used by pre-school children' *Journal of Experimental Child Psychology*, 35, pp.93-110

Hillman (1993) 'Children, Transport and the Quality of Life', Policy Studies Institute

OFSTED (1996) *Primary Subject Guidance*, (Guidance for inspecting subjects and areas of learning in primary and nursery schools)

Palmer, J. (1993) 'From Santa Claus to sustainability: emergent understanding of concepts and issues in Environmental Science' *International Journal of Science Education*, 15(5), pp. 487-496

SCAA (1996) *Desirable Outcomes for Children's Learning on Entering Compulsory Education.* SCAA and DfEE

Somerville, S. and Bryant, P. (1985) 'Young children's use of spatial co-ordinates', in *Child Development*, 56, pp. 604-613

Stillwell, R. and Spencer, C. (1974) 'Children's early preferences for other nations and their subsequent acquisition of knowledge about those nations' *European Journal of Social Psychology*, 3, 3, pp. 345-349

Storm, M. (1984) Teaching about minorities, N. Fyson (ed.) *The Development Puzzle*, Sevenoaks: Hodder and Stoughton/CWDE

West, J. (1981) 'Children's awareness of the past', Keele University: unpublished PhD thesis

Wiegand, P. (1991) 'The known world of the primary school' *Geography*, 76, 2, pp.143-149

Wiegand, P. (1993) *Children and Primary Geography*, London: Cassell

PART III

CROSS-CURRICULAR LEARNING

CHAPTER 9

FOSTERING CREATIVE DEVELOPMENT

Bernadette Duffy

Introduction

Creative development is of immense importance in all areas of learning and development. It is identified as a distinct area of learning in the Desirable Learning Outcomes (SCAA, 1996) and while there is no subject called creativity in the National Curriculum, the creative process involving exploration, discovery, reflection and expression is part of all subjects. Creativity is seen as a good thing and has a long tradition in early childhood settings. Froebel in the nineteenth century associated creativity with the inner life of the child –

> We become truly Godlike in diligence and industry, in working and doing, which are accompanied by the clear perception or even the vaguest feeling that thereby we represent the inner in the outer... (Froebel,1826, p. 31).

And we are still urged to promote creativity by:

- Her Majesty's Inspectorate 1989:
  Teaching should encourage children 'to be imaginative and creative'
  (Aspects of Primary Education; The Education of Children Under Five p.8)

- The School Curriculum and Assessment Authority 1996:
  Settings must ensure 'the development of children's imagination and their ability to communicate and to express ideas in creative ways'
  (Desirable Outcomes for Children's Learning On Entry to Compulsory Education p.4)

- The Department for Education 1995:

'pupils should be taught the creative, imaginative and practical skills they need to express ideas and feelings, record observation, design and make images and artefacts' (Art Programme of Study in the National Curriculum p.2)

- National Vocational Qualifications in Child Care and Education 1991: Candidates must know how to 'Set out natural and other materials for creative play' and 'Help children to express their imagination and creativity' (Council for Awards in Child Care and Education).

Yet as Bruner (1986) has argued, society has placed a greater value on logical and systematic thought. This can lead to over-emphasising the ability to retain and repeat facts, to be impartial, dispassionate and detached. When only the rational aspects of learning and development are stressed we deprive ourselves of the full range of the human ability to think, and creativity does not receive the attention it deserves.

This chapter examines the following issues:

- why creativity is important for society and children

- defining and recognising creativity

- the creative process

- the cross-curricular nature of the creative process

- designing an environment which encourages the creative process

- evaluating the creative process

The importance of creativity for society and young children

Society has always needed people who are creative and imaginative, people who are able to come up with creative solutions to problems and imaginatively combine previously unconnected ideas and skills. The desire to be creative, to represent and share our experiences with others, seems to be a basic human characteristic that has existed throughout history in all communities. From earliest times human beings have made their mark using the materials available to them – prehistoric cave paintings, for instance. Creation myths devised by religious and cultural groups also reflect this desire. Some of them use the imagery of human creativity to express divine creativity (Lynch, 1992). The myths emphasise the desire to create, the pleasure in the process and the sense of ownership towards the created, and these are reflected in our own experience of creativity. We are born with the need to share and understand the ideas, thoughts and feelings of others and from this need have developed the representations of our culture, such as the visual and performing arts (Trevarthen, 1995).

The world we live in is changing rapidly. We do not know the challenges that will face the children we work with in their adult lives, but we do know that in order to meet these challenges children will need to be creative. Creative and imaginative experiences give us the opportunity to:

- develop the full range of human potential

- improve our capacity for thought, action and communication

- nurture our feelings and sensibilities

- extend our physical and perceptual skills

- explore values

- understand our own and other cultures
  (Calouste Gulbenkian, 1982)

It is not only for the sake of future society that we need to educate young children in ways that emphasise and encourage their creativity – education in the early years is valid in its own right. By encouraging creativity we are promoting children's ability to explore and comprehend their world, to respond and represent their perceptions. We are increasing their opportunities to make new connections, reach new understandings and create new meanings. The creative process helps children to experience beauty and lasting value, express their cultural heritage and increase their understanding of other cultures. It helps them to solve problems and gain command and it promotes self-esteem.

Children need to *represent* their experiences, feelings and ideas if they are to preserve them and share them with others. When we represent we make an object or symbol stand for something else; for example, spoken language is a form of symbolic representation with words standing for something in the real world. Matthews (1994) stresses the significance of children acquiring this ability. From it springs the understanding to comprehend other forms of symbolic representation such as written language and mathematics. Once children can separate objects and actions from their meaning in the real world and give them new meanings they are no longer tied to the concrete world and start to think in an abstract way. For example, if they can pretend that a stick is no longer a stick but is to be used as if it were a pencil, they can start to understand that the marks 'c-a-t' on a page, which do not look or sound like a cat, can be used to represent a cat.

Children use their creative representations to communicate and express their thoughts in non-verbal and pre-verbal ways. Different forms of representation enable them to address problems in various ways and gain new insights. They may:

- draw a picture or diagram

- describe an experience in words – verbally or in writing

- use role-play to act out a situation

- build a model using blocks or other materials

- use movement and dance to express an emotion

- paint a picture

- compose a piece of music

Access to creative and imaginative experiences is not only for the children who are as gifted. Everyone has entitlement to a wide range of experience and to reach his or her full potential. But some children find that their access is limited due to the different values society gives to different groups of people based on their race, religion, culture, class and ethnicity, gender, or special educational needs. Children are aware of the values and judgements of the adults around them from a young age. The distorted opinions that develop from exposure to beliefs that are based on prejudice and discrimination will stay with them.

The range of abilities evident in any group of children make it unwise simply to assume competence, or lack of it, on the basis of membership of a certain group. The abilities children display may be the result of innate ability but can also be the outcome of encouragement from the adults around them. For example, some groups of Chinese children have highly developed drawing skills at an early age due to the value placed on drawing and early instruction in these skills by the communities in which they live (Cox, 1992). Our challenge is to confront stereotypes that limit access, and instead offer experiences which extend the horizons of all children.

Defining and recognising creativity

We need to develop definitions of creativity that

- are not élitist

- recognise that all children have the ability to be creative and imaginative

- makes the most of the talents of all children

- embrace the idea that all children need opportunities to play with ideas, and

- acknowledge the importance of an environment which encourages and values creativity

But defining creativity can be difficult. Definitions may limit creativity to the production of an artefact such as a painting. They may restrict creativity to the 'arts', as only to do with painting or music or simply a skill – something which can be taught by means of instruction. Such notions limit creativity to the gifted few or a view that certain groups of people are naturally creative.

The Oxford Dictionary defines creativity as: 'to create – to bring into existence' while Parnes (1963 p5) describes it as 'a thinking and responding process that involves connecting with our previous experience, responding to stimuli (objects, symbols, ideas, people, situations) and generally at least one unique combination'. As McKellar (1957) points out, creativity does not occur in a vacuum. All creative thought has external sources, which may be remote or recent, conscious or unconscious. The creative element is in connecting and re-arranging information from these sources.

Creativity involves

- the ability to see things in fresh ways

- learning from past experiences and relating this learning to new situations

- thinking along unorthodox lines and breaking barriers

- using non-traditional approaches to solving problems

- going further than the information given

- creating something unique or original

Most of the things children discover and create are not original to society. They have been discovered or created before but they are new to the child. Children are being creative when they make a connection that is new to them. I would define creativity as connecting the previously unconnected in ways that are new and meaningful to the individual concerned.

The creative process

The creative process involves selection, reasoning and hard thinking. It involves a condensation of perceptual information and its transformation into a new form (McKellar, 1957). During this process we need to saturate ourselves with ideas, to become so familiar with the concepts involved in the particular problem that we are solving that we can recall them automatically.

Cecil, Gray, Thornburgh and Ispa (1985) offer us a model of the creative process that can be used to support the creative process, whether it relates to ideas or equipment or a combination of both. There are four levels in this process:

- Curiosity or what is it? Children become aware of a problem, a new idea or pieces of information. They are alert, interested and want to know more. Their attention has been caught.

- Exploration or what can and does it do? Children can be observed actively investigating objects, events or ideas. They are often using all their senses to gather information and their existing knowledge and understanding to identify connections, similarities and differences. Watching others can also be part of their investigation.

- Play or what can I do with this? Children initiate a period of total immersion characterised by spontaneity and often without clear final objectives. As there is little or no focus on a predetermined product they are free to examine all kinds of detail during this period that they might have missed if they had been concentrating on the end product. This is an opportunity to practise and consolidate the skills and knowledge they have acquired in the earlier levels. It is also an opportunity to ponder and allow ideas to incubate. This may take place over a number of days or minutes.

- Creativity or what can I create or invent? Children have an insight into the problem, a moment of illumination. They discover uncommon or new approaches to the materials or problem they are investigating; they take risks and make new connections. This leads to a possible solution or a meaningful connection. This is the moment of creativity.

These levels overlap and evolve out of each other. During the process children move backward and forward in their thinking – it is not a linear approach. Frequently the solution or grasp of an idea will lead them on to a new idea or problem – a new challenge to overcome.

The cross curricular nature of the creative process

Creativity is important in its own right and also because it fosters the development of the whole child by promoting learning across the curriculum. Creativity is part of every subject area.

The creative process in science and technology

The growth of scientific and technological ways of knowing has been associated with the undervaluing of and even conflict with creativity. But science and technology require the ability to think creatively as much as any of the arts subjects traditionally associated with creativity (Heckscher, 1966). Behind every scientific or technological discovery is a moment of connection, a moment of inspiration and creativity. There should be no conflict between the two modes of thinking, between the logical and the intuitive. It is

> **Example**
>
> Victor, aged 5 years, was part of a group of children discussing a forthcoming visit to a farm during which they would find out how milk was made into cheese. The children were encouraged to explore a range of possibilities, and various solutions were suggested. Some thought that it was to do with magic, while others remembered their own experience of producing butter by shaking cream in a jam jar and thought that this was what happened. Victor listened carefully and commented that it had taken a long time to shake the cream and the farmer must have a quicker way. After this discussion Victor went away to ponder the problem and created his own diagram of a cheese-making machine with tubes that lead from the cow's udder to a shaking machine to create the cheese. Victor's machine drew on his knowledge of butter making and his under-standing of machines; he was able to combine these items of information to create his own solution.

not a case of either/or: it is both. They offer complementary views and, when combined, advance our understanding of the world in which we live and our ability to respond creatively to its challenges.

The cheese-making machine is a lovely example of technology. In science it could be the spontaneous remarks by a child that a rose and a daisy are both flowers. The child is demonstrating scientific creativity, without having specifically been taught it – she has applied her previous knowledge of similar items called 'flowers' and applied an established botanical taxonomy to these two new (to her) specimens.

> **Example**
>
> Seeing patterns is at the heart of mathematics. A group of 4 year olds had been exploring patterns with their teacher. They became aware that repetition is the key to pattern and began to identify patterns in the environment, for example, the waltz rhythm in music '1,2,3, 1,2,3, 1,2,3,' – and to create their own patterns, such as how they organised the fruit snack: apple, orange, banana, pear, apple, orange, banana, pear... While examining the number square two of the children discovered another pattern: the number at the end of each row ended with zero – 10,20,30,40... No one had drawn the children's attention to this fact; they had used their knowledge of number and their growing awareness of pattern to connect the previously unconnected in a way that was new and meaningful to them.

The creative process in mathematics

Mathematics and creativity are sometimes seen as mutually exclusive. The way many of us were taught mathematics as children, with emphasis on reproducing facts rather than creating our own understandings, has left us with feelings of confusion and sometimes a distinct lack of enthusiasm! We can easily pass on these feelings and views of mathematics to the children in our care. But creativity is very much part of mathematics. Grey's work revealed that the children who were successful mathematicians were those who had learnt how to develop new facts from old in a flexible way (Grey, 1997) – in other words they were creative.

Munn found that children rarely understood adult purposes of counting before they went to school. For young children counting meant simply to recite the words in the correct order. The quantitative goal was missing from their understanding. Children need time and opportunities to develop their own understandings (Munn, 1997). 'Children who are used to organising themselves in play and learning activities are more likely to become confident and creative mathematicians' (Gifts, 1993 p.147).

The creative process in literacy

The creative process is vital to literacy and approaches which emphasise the mechanics of reading and writing to the exclusion of creativity will limit children's development as readers and writers. Engle (1995) makes the link between children's imaginative play and the development of their story

---

Example

Laura, 3 years and 1 month, was fascinated by fairy tales. Her interest had been supported by her parents and key worker at the centre she attended. Laura had spent much of the previous week engaged in acting out her own versions of fairy tales and at the suggestion of her key worker was recording these in a book she had made. She wrote various letters to which she ascribed meaning and read these to the adult. She illustrated the story as she went. Her story told of a little girl who wanted to be a princess. To achieve this she needed a princess dress. But her mother would only let her have a workaday dress and told her that she was only a little girl, not a princess and it was time for bed. Laura drew together elements from her understanding of real life – the time scale and sequence of events are based on the familiar daily routine of her life – and used her knowledge of fairy tales such as Cinderella and Beauty and the Beast to create her own story with its own meaning.

making skills. Imaginative play scenarios act as one of the sources of the stories children tell and in turn the stories they create inform their imaginative play, providing a structure which allows children to guide one another in their play (Engel, 1995). For Chukovsky there is a strong link between exposure to fairy tales and the development of creativity and the future belongs to those who do not rein in their imagination (Chukovsky, 1963).

Payley points out that children reveal themselves through the stories and characters they act out. The stories children create are one way of communicating their unique experience of the world. Young children's stories address their pressing concerns, urgent questions and passions; this is what makes the children eloquent (Payley, 1986). Without the creative element children are unable to do this. 'Fantasy is the most valuable attribute of the human mind and it should be diligently nurtured from early childhood' (Chukovsky, 1963 p.115).

Example

Joe, aged 4 years and 3 months, was engaged in painting for his parents – 'It's a picture of a happy sun shining on a field of dancing flowers'. While the images of the sun and flowers he used owed much to observation of his older friend's drawings, the composition was all his own. Joe mixed the exact shade he wanted for each flower and placed it with great care. The arrangements of the petals varied as he tried to make each turn towards the smiling sun. The result was an image that was unique to Joe.

Creativity as part of the performing and visual arts

Creativity is traditionally associated with the visual and performing arts, such as drawing and painting, dance and music. These experiences are often seen as the key to creative development. But too often the very activities that are labelled as creative in schools, nurseries and at home are more about filling time, learning a set of techniques or decoration rather than true creativity. Pre-printed, adult directed and mass-produced artwork does not lead to creativity but to reproduction. When we are engaged in reproduction we use a single source of information and the result is predictable. When we are being creative we use information from a variety of sources which are fused together to produce an integrated whole. These sources may include images that other people have created but they are combined with information from other sources, including our imagination. Simply copying the image of another is reproduction not creativity (McKellar, 1957).

Children's access to the creative process can be curtailed for a variety of reasons. Adults may confuse freedom of expression with the freedom to do whatever one wishes and fear that anarchy will result! But, as we have seen, the creative process is characterised by a high degree of self-discipline, concentration and persistence. The freedom to explore ideas freely must be based on respect for oneself and others. Another problem can be curriculum demands, especially at Key Stage 1. As children get older it can seem that much of the school day is taken up with the core subjects, and that creativity and imagination are seen as a luxury or extra to be fitted in when the core curriculum has been delivered. When time is limited it can appear that the best solution is to pre-package children's learning to ensure that the whole curriculum is covered and limit or remove opportunities for children to be creative. However, we do this at our peril. Without the opportunity to engage in the creative process in all areas of learning, children will not reach their full potential. We must ensure that children have the time and space for their sakes and for that of society.

Designing an environment which encourages the creative process

If we want children to express their imagination we need to provide an environment in which they can do this. In designing this environment we need to think about the role of the adult, the importance of other children and also the physical environment.

Adults' attitudes are crucial to the development of creativity in young children. But what exactly is our role? Should we become directly involved or would this stifle children's potential? Should we provide the equipment and materials and stand back or would this result in a lack of progress and challenge? How do we balance the danger of over-direction against anxieties about becoming involved? Often our own early childhood experiences can hinder us. We may have been told that we were no good at art or music. The embarrassment, anxieties and fears that these responses to our early imaginative representations evoke can re-surface in later life. Do we have the ability to support young children's development? The history of art education illuminates the dilemma.

Pickering (1976) explains that in the last century children were viewed as inept artists who needed to be taught the skills and techniques that would enable them to produce artwork that met adult expectations and purposes. One has only to look at the carefully crafted samplers produced by girls from a relatively young age to see this approach in action.

The work of art educators such as Cizek (Viola, 1937) and Richardson (1948), challenged this view and led to a change in attitude. They both believed that children were artists in their own right who should not be forced or pressed to produce images to meet adult expectations and that self-expression was important. These views have led to a concern that by intervening in children's imaginative processes adults might harm or even destroy children's free expression by imposing on them adult views and pre-occupations. If we intervene with a view that the purpose of art is to produce an image that is as realistic as possible and therefore think of children as failed realists, we may do great harm by imposing inappropriate expectations which do not match children's developmental stages.

However Cox (1992) has criticised some of the approaches to art education that have developed from the work of Cizek and Richardson. She argues against approaches based on the view that development and learning take care of themselves. The result can be a strategy that is so 'hands off' that it leaves children without the skills and knowledge to progress, with the consequence that they become frustrated. Too often we hear older children and adults say 'I'm no good at art or music, I can't draw or sing'. Their initial delight in drawing, construction, painting, music making and role-play changes to reluctance and uncertainty.

Children need to interact with other people if their learning is to progress. They want to share their imaginative representations with adults and adults can help them increase their ability to communicate their thoughts, feelings and ideas through their representations. Kindler (1995) observed children in her son's day-care centre. She found that though the area was well supplied with a variety of materials the children took little advantage of them. Only when adults were physically present in the area and became involved with the children did the children's participation, concentration and exploration increase. Her conclusion was that the mere availability of materials is not enough; adult input is essential.

Our interventions should support and extend children's learning and development by adding the information or skill they need at the point they need it. Our role is to create conditions within which children are inspired to be imaginative and to develop children's imagination and creativity through our interactions with them.

The way we organise and use the available space inside and out is crucial in creating opportunities for children to express themselves. Children need sufficient space to work and they need easily accessible resources to make the best use of experiences offered to them. The space will vary greatly. It may be in a home or in a centre-based setting. Each setting will offer its own possibilities. We need to look at each setting and maximise its potential.

Creativity is to some degree resource led. The range of resources and organisation we provide will determine what and how the children can create and how creative they can be. Our organisation of space and resources will largely determine what children can do.

While space and resources will vary between settings it is important that whatever is available is organised in a tidy way. It is frustrating for children and adults if they are delayed and possibly distracted because they cannot find a resource or piece of equipment at a crucial moment. The work areas of artists and crafts people are usually extremely well organised, everything easy to locate and readily at hand. McKellar (1957) explains that the arrangement of the physical space can aid concentration, create a mood conducive to creativity and increase motivation.

The creative process takes time. Children need time to experiment and explore, to play and practise, to try new ideas and modify their representations in response to the feedback they get. This means that we need to think about the organisation of the time available. Is the session organised in a way that allows for uninterrupted exploration and minimises interruptions? Is there an appropriate balance between child and adult initiated activity? Is there time for children to work alone, and/or with other children and with adults? Can explorations continue over time – from morning to afternoon; from day to day; over weeks; allowing children to refine and develop their ideas and representations?

The importance of peers cannot be overstressed, and how children are organised will determine the opportunities they have to work with a variety of children in groups of different sizes. Same and cross-age groups have different characteristics. Working in cross-age groups enables younger children to observe and learn from more experienced learners, while the opportunity to scaffold the learning of younger children helps the older children to clarify their thinking. Children of the same age or stage of development will often have similar interests and a desire to explore these together. The size of the group also has an impact: a pair might exchange ideas and work together, while group of three or four may precipitate the type of conflicts that can stimulate new connections and creativity. Experiences such as these help children to become receptive to the ideas of others (Edwards, Gandini and Foreman, 1995).

Exploring the local environment and sharing the creative and imaginative representations of adults in the community inducts children into their own culture, while exposure to the representations of other communities introduces them to cultures other than their own. We must nurture and inspire them by widening their horizons.

Evaluating the creative process

Creativity can occur at any age. It is about connecting the previously unconnected. As we learn and develop our ability to make connections increases, we have more information to combine and more skills to employ. Although each child is unique, children do go through recognisable and similar stages in their development. If we know the likely pattern of development we will be better able to assess the children we are responsible for and so meet their needs and interests.

Stages of development should not be seen as a ladder. Children do not start at the first rung and progress until they reach the top. The stages of development are to assist us, the adults. They help us to support children's learning by being aware of their possible interests and needs at different stages in their development. Nor are they tick-lists to measure children against. Learning influences creativity and experience, and children of the same age may show a marked variation in their abilities. Children will revisit earlier stages of development and in early stages will show elements of later learning, and children with special educational needs may take longer to move through the stages.

In some settings assessments and evaluations will be made with reference to Desirable Outcomes for Children's Learning and to the National Curriculum. The creative process may result in a work product, an observation of the process the children went through, or a transcript of their comments. We can analyse and assess these in a number of ways:

- What does the example tell us about the children's understanding of the world, their thoughts or feelings?

- What have the children achieved? How does it match with the aims we identified at the planning stage?

- What is the children's assessment of the experience? What do they think they have achieved?

- What knowledge, attitudes and skills have the children shown in their use of materials and equipment that they have not demonstrated before?

- Which elements of art, music, science, maths... have they used and to what effect?

- How have the children worked individually or as part of a group?

- How has their use of materials or ideas demonstrated the creative process?

- What new connections have they made?

- What is their actual level of development and how do we help them to progress to the next stage?

- What have we, the adults achieved? How did our plans work in practice?

Children's intentions are not always recognised by adult definitions and evaluations. So it is essential to involve children in the assessment and planning of their work. We need to find out from them what their intentions were. Why have they used materials or ideas in that particular way? Does the result satisfy them, and are they happy with it? What would they like to do or know next? Obviously children's ability to engage in conversations of this sort develops as they mature. But with the support of a well-known and receptive adult children can start to take part in this process from an early age. Our comments are most useful when they help children to recognise the elements they have used in their representation and make links between their use of these elements and the use that others have made of them. A trusting relationship, honesty and a shared understanding with an adult provides the security children need to discuss their representations, reflect on their learning and identify the next step.

Children's homes and family life often provide the ideas and themes that are reflected in their creative and imaginative representations. For this reason alone adults who work with children other than their own need to involve parents in their assessment and planning of children's experiences. Without the input of parents we will lack access to these major influences on children's representations and our assessments will be partial.

Conclusion

Children's opportunities to explore freely are being increasingly curtailed. Parents' concerns about safety may mean that children are no longer able to play freely in streets or parks unless adults supervise them closely. To compensate for the decrease in children's free play opportunities there has been an increase in organised activity for them. Children often attend a variety of dance, music and drama groups from a young age. These are frequently adult directed and do not allow children the time and space to explore and create in their own ways. We need to find ways to reverse this trend and use our creativity to secure for children the opportunities they need.

Acknowledgements

Many thanks to Deva Priya for her help with this chapter. The ideas in this chapter are further developed in Duffy, B (1998) *Supporting Creativity and Imagination in the Early Years*, Buckingham: Open University Press.

Recommended Texts

Cecil, L. M., Gray, M.M., Thornburg, K.R., and Ispa, J. (1985) Curiosity – exploration – play: the early childhood mosaic, *Early Child Development and Care* Vol.19 pp 199-217.
This article describes the creative process and shows how it can be used in early childhood education.

Mc Kellar, P. (1957] *Imagination and thinking* London: Cohen and West.
Explores the nature of creativity and imagination.

References

Bruner, J. (1986) *Actual Minds, Possible Worlds,* Harvard: Harvard University Press

Gulbenkian, Calouste (1982) *The Arts in School,* London: Calouste Gulbenkian Foundation

Cecil, L. M., Gray, M.M., Thornburg, K.R., and Ispa, J. (1985) Curiosity – exploration – play: the early childhood mosaic, *Early Child Development and Care* Vol.19 pp 199-217

Chukovsky, K. (1963) *From two to five*, California: University of California Press

Council for Awards in Child Care and Education (1991) *National Qualifications in Child Care and Education*, St Albans, Herts: CACHE

Cox, M. (1992) *Children's Drawings*, London: Penguin

Department for Education and School Curriculum and Assessment Authority (1996) *The National Curriculum*, London: HMSO

SCAA (1996) *Desirable Outcomes for Children's Learning on Entry to Compulsory Education*, London: SCAA and DfEE

Edwards, C., Gandini, L., and Foreman, G. (Ed) *The Hundred Languages of Children*, New Jersey: Ablex

Engle, S. (1995) *The Stories Children Tell: Making sense of the narratives of childhood*, New York: W.H.Freeman

Froebel, F. (1826) *The Education of Man*, New York: Appleton

Grey, E. (1997) 'Compressing the counting process: developing a flexible interpretation of symbols', Thompson, I. *Teaching and learning early number*, Buckingham: Open University Press

Griffiths, (1993) 'Mathematics and play', Moyles, J. *The Excellence of play*, Buckingham: Open University Press

Her Majesty's Inspectorate (1989) *Aspects of Primary Education, the education of children under five*, London: HMSO

Heckscher, A. (1966) The child's world: Today and Tomorrow, Lewis, H. (ed.) *Child Art at the Beginning of Self Affirmation*: London: Diabolo Press

Kindler, A. (1995) Significance of Adult Input in Early Childhood Artistic Development, Thompson (Ed.) *The Visual Arts and Early Childhood*, Washington: National Association for the Education of Children

Lynch, M. (1992) *Creation Myths*, London: West London Institute of Higher Education

Matthews, J. (1994) *Helping children to draw and paint in early childhood*, London: Hodder and Stoughton

Munn, P. (1997) Children's beliefs about counting, Thompson, I. *Teaching and learning early number* Buckingham: Open University Press

McKellar, P. (1957) *Imagination and thinking*, London: Cohen and West

Parnes, S. (1963) Development of individual creative talent, Tylor C.W. and Barrons F. (Eds.) *Scientific Creativity its recognition and development,* New York: Wiley

Paley, V.G. (1986) On listening to what children say, *Harvard Educational Review* Vol: 56 No.2 May 1986

Pickering, J. (1976) Visual education for young children, Brothwell, D. *Investigations into the nature of visual art*, London: Thames and Hudson

Richardson, M. (1948) *Art and the child*, London: University of London Press

Trevarthen, C. (1995) The Child's Need to Learn a Culture, *Children and Society* Vol: 9 No.1 pp 5-19

Viola, W. (1937) *Child Art and Frank Cizek,* Austria: Austrian Junior Red Cross

CHAPTER 10

THINKING ABOUT ME AND THEM: PERSONAL AND SOCIAL DEVELOPMENT

Rosemary Roberts

■ Introduction

This chapter is in two parts. The first part covers the main aspects of a personal and social curriculum and the second looks at the practical implications of those aspects. Both offer 'starting points' for action.

The process of children's personal and social development is essentially interactive, involving relationships and interactions with other people. The moral and spiritual dimensions of children's lives are very closely linked to the interactive nature of personal and social development. In an uncertain moral and spiritual climate it is especially relevant for early childhood educators to pay attention to this area of children's development. The book edited by Ron Best *Education, Spirituality and the Whole Child* (1996) is extremely helpful. Although this chapter is primarily about personal and social development, much – although of course not all – of the content relates also to moral and spiritual development.

Any exploration of the place of these areas of development in early childhood education needs to focus on what they mean, but first we must be clear about the *purposes* of early childhood education and how this area of the curriculum contributes to those purposes. The central questions relate not only to the value of personal and social development in its own right, but also to its cross-curricular nature and its crucial role in underpinning the rest of the curriculum.

There is still considerable debate about the purposes of early childhood education. Is the priority to meet the current developmental needs of young children? Or is it to prepare them for subsequent learning? Or is it to learn more knowledge and skills at an earlier age? Let us assume that these purposes are all desirable, and that any curriculum and pedagogy must avoid their being mutually exclusive.

Katz (1995) proposes four main goals for education: knowledge, skills, dispositions and feelings. While the first two are familiar territory in curriculum documentation and implementation, the others generally receive hardly more than a passing reference, particularly once children enter statutory education and the requirements of a national curriculum take priority. Yet we all know, both as educators and learners, that dispositions and feelings are fundamental to the likelihood of success in relation to acquiring knowledge and skills. That personal and social development as described below essentially relates to dispositions and feelings is a strong argument for its inclusion at the *heart* of any curriculum and especially for the early years when a child's sense of self, of others, and of the environment is at such a formative and vulnerable stage.

The argument for placing personal and social education at the heart of the curriculum relates not only to children's needs in these early years, but also to preparation for later learning. An examination of the impact of early learning on children's later development concludes that: 'The most important learning in pre-school concerns aspiration, task commitment, social skills and feelings of efficacy' (Sylva, 1994). She makes a strong case that children's dispositions and feelings are at the heart of their ability to learn successfully. Personal and social development is central to children's fulfilment as people, and to their ability to be successful learners. In our concerted effort to raise children's educational attainment, it is literally of the *first* importance that we consider how we support that development in an informed, effective and cross-curricular way. (J. and I. Siraj-Blatchford, 1995.)

■ What are the aspects of a personal and social curriculum?

Four perspectives will be considered here, together with some practical starting points relating to strategies: developing a sense of self, relationships with others, awareness of the cultural and physical environment, and linking feelings and learning dispositions.

1. Developing a sense of self

Understanding ourselves is a life-long process. For all of us – adults and children – the 'mirroring' process of perceiving ourselves through the eyes of others begins at birth, and its early childhood roots are all-important (Roberts, 1995). The mother-infant relationship is naturally of great importance (Miller, 1992). Relationships with other 'significant' adults cannot be underestimated (Harris, 1989), and the effects of peer group perceptions and friendships are also significant (Dunn, 1995 and Paley, 1992).

■ *Starting points*

Here are four starting points for people who are exploring ways of working to support children's developing sense of self.

About the first stage of the 'mirror' process ...

How young children see themselves is significantly affected by the way their 'important' people approach them and respond to them. For every child, consciously or unconsciously, an all-important question is 'Am I acceptable, am I lovable?' The approaches and responses of people around them profoundly influence children's developing sense of self – positively or negatively.

About body language ...

An important element of these early exchanges of information between children and other people is the use of body language. In adulthood, and in various cultures, the extent to which we retain the use of our original language – body language – varies enormously. For young children, however, it should be remembered that body language is, to a large extent, *still* their main language; especially in relation to emotional matters. This is how they understand how we adults feel, and what we mean. How we look, and the *way* in which something is said, is likely to mean more to a young child than the words themselves.

About responsibility and self-respect ...

Children's confidence and independence depends on their ability to see themselves as reasonably competent and responsible. This ability depends in part on whether other people already perceive them in this way. (It is very hard to think of oneself as competent if no-one else has ever explicitly done so.) Learning to be responsible happens as a result of being given responsibility – another instance of the interactional nature of the development of a positive (or negative) sense of self. Children cannot become responsible beings on their own, they need adults to hand over to them real respon-sibilities through which they can learn. It is a complex process, in which much of the responsibility for a child's progress rests with the adult! As for self-respect, this is another instance of the way in which children learn behaviours and dispositions from their important adults. When parents or other 'significant' people respect children, children learn to respect them-selves – and each other.

About managing difficult feelings and behaviour ...

In the normal course of events most young children have a good deal to con-tend with in the way of loss, much of which generates pain, anxiety or anger. Although losing the safety of the womb and the comfort of the breast or bottle will not be remembered consciously, subsequent experiences of loss – for instance of important people coming and going; of an outgrown cot, coat, or cuddly toy; of relinquishing baby status to a new baby or losing a friend to a rival; or going from nursery to school – all of these can be seen as mile-stones of growing up, where the new alternative may well be preferable. But gain and loss can be as close as love and hate, and in early childhood just as challenging to manage. In addition there is so much that is new and strange for young children about the world that they feel overwhelmed at times and react accordingly.

One of the hardest things that parents and other adults who live and work with young children have to cope with is all the times when children com-plain, whinge or argue. Generally we do not listen readily when children behave like this, and the message they tend to get from us is that we are find-ing them unacceptable. This is extremely threatening for them, and it is a measure of their desperation that so many children keep up their whinging for so long! Most are unable to distinguish between the feeling itself and their expression of it so unfortunately what they learn well before adolescence is that feelings of pain, anxiety and anger are bad things to have, and that it is best to hide them.

There are two helpful approaches here. Firstly, adults can try and listen care-fully to children's verbal protests. Young children can manage pain, anxiety and anger more easily if they know that adults accept how they feel; and it is important to remember that it is possible for adults to *listen and sympathise* with children's feelings, *without* becoming committed to a particular course of *action.*

Secondly, children need to know that their 'important' adults accept *them* un-conditionally, even when their *behaviour* is not acceptable. If children are behaving in challenging ways, they need to know that it is their *behaviour* that is deplored, not the children themselves (Siraj-Blatchford, 1994). In this way they can retain their self-respect and confidence, which enables them to review their behaviour – whether it is about how they relate to others and function in a group, about their treatment of property or the environment, or about any other personal, social, moral or spiritual issue.

2. Relationships with others

Many young children show tolerance and co-operation, turn-taking and sharing, sensitivity to others and a sense of justice when they play together. Although these characteristics may often be lacking in adult contexts, one has only to observe children playing freely in an early years setting to see astonishing evidence in some children of the extent to which they can do these things at an early age. On the other hand, the same observations yield evidence of how challenging our expectations of young children are in this regard, and how very difficult it is for some children to meet those expectations. In addition, perhaps it is appropriate to wonder what sort of role models children are given in the patterns of our adult relationships and interactions in society generally. Do we sometimes expect more of young children than we do of ourselves?

■ *Starting points*

About the second stage of the 'mirror' process ...

Children gradually learn how to behave towards others as a result of how others behave towards them. This applies not only to their friends, but also – possibly even more so – to their 'significant' adults.

About staff as models for children ...

Staff in early childhood education settings have constant opportunity to give children experiences of tolerance, co-operation, sharing and turn-taking, sensitivity and justice. The most powerful way that staff can do this is by their own example, in the ways in which they treat each other, as well as the children in their care. Children cannot be expected to give to others what they themselves have never had.

About values ... caught or taught?

Similarly, the effective transmission of values in early childhood education is essentially a modelling process. Concepts of individual worth, honesty, right and wrong, justice, entitlement and collective endeavour are within the scope of young children's understanding, provided they experience these things in a concrete way. Because these concepts must be 'caught' rather than taught, the implications for staff in early childhood education are significant. The adults' own actions, their relationships with others, their response to the environment and their commitment to society needs to be of the highest standards. Although this sounds daunting, it can be an exciting challenge for any staff community and makes for enormous job satisfaction.

About learning the consequences of actions ...

If children are to learn about the consequences of their actions towards others, it is not the job of staff to protect them from the consequences any more than is necessary for their physical and emotional safety. On the other hand, staff do have a very important role to play in helping children to reflect on their actions and to recognise and value achievements, and they can support children in trying alternatives when appropriate.

About the need to plan for this learning, and to assess outcomes ...

Children will have already learned much about the possibilities of tolerance, co-operation, sharing and turn-taking, sensitivity and justice at home. Parents – experts about their own children – can help enormously by sharing information and priorities with staff. Specific arrangements for staff and individual parents to spend time together are essential for this process of partnership to be effective. As well as acknowledging the importance of such home learning, staff can build on it by planning for children's learning in this area. Practitioners may need to check how this planning actually takes place, whether observations are systematically achieved, and by what criteria children's progress is judged.

3. Awareness of the cultural and physical environment

This perspective involves children's explorations of technology; dimensions of place and time in the natural world; knowledge about other people and their beliefs and value systems; and the various ways in which feelings, ideas and experiences are represented in play and in the creative and expressive arts.

■ Starting points

About other chapters in this book ...

The aspects of the early years curriculum relating to the cultural and physical environment are considered in detail here in Chapters 7, 8 and 9, where much helpful material can be found. It is especially through these areas of knowledge and investigation that children can develop positive perceptions and responses to differences, respect and responsibility for the natural and man-made world, and the ability to express feelings of wonder, joy and sorrow in relation to their experiences of the world.

About a cross-curricular approach ...

A cross-curricular approach is the means whereby children develop their sensitivity to others, their respect for other cultures and beliefs, their care and concern for things, property and the environment, and their ability to understand and contribute to the various ways in which children and adults represent the world. It can be argued (and probably corroborated by the evidence of a thousand adult memories) that completely cross-curricular activities – such as discovering the uses and fascinations of pulleys, digging together in the earth for worms or 'archaeological' fragments, inventing feasts for friends, examining climbing-frame spider's webs on blindingly beautiful frosty mornings, representing friendships in glorious bright slippery paint – are the ones that 'stretch the mind and grow the soul' ... and stay in the memory.

4. Linking emotions and learning dispositions

Children's self-esteem is a key factor not only for their well-being but also for learning outcomes. Indeed it can be argued that most of the desirable outcomes of personal and social education in the early years are likely to fall into place for certain children: those with high self-esteem based on a realistic awareness of their own efforts and achievements. The development of high self-esteem – better termed positive self-concept – is therefore an appropriate priority in any consideration of personal and social development, both for its own sake and for its impact on learning.

Positive self-concept is largely dependent on two of the theoretical perspectives of personal and social development: the sense of self, and relationships with others. There is a third perspective in the development of positive self-concept mentioned earlier which is crucial to cognitive development: learning dispositions. A disposition may be defined as 'a tendency to exhibit frequently, consciously and voluntarily a pattern of behaviour that is directed to a broad goal' (Katz, 1993). Such patterns of behaviour can be positive or negative, for example: persistence at a task; a disposition to curiosity, or generosity, or meanness; or the tendency to read, or to solve problems.

The characteristics of children who are disposed to learn are likely to include all or most of the following, the regular use of which can be termed dispositions: the ability to communicate well, explore, experiment, listen well, concentrate, persevere, ask for help, learn from mistakes, show independence, initiate ideas, solve problems, and reflect. These are the children who tend to say 'I can' rather than 'I can't', and who may be said to have a generally positive disposition to learn. They are also the children who tend to have a positive self-concept.

■ Starting points

About self-esteem ...

Children with high self-esteem are more likely to exhibit 'well-being' and learn successfully than children with low self-esteem.

High self-esteem thrives especially on four factors:

- acceptance: a concept dependent on the mirroring process (see above, this chapter)

- adults dealing positively with normal 'bad' feelings (see above, this chapter)

- adults setting limits clearly and consistently, so that children feel secure (see below, this chapter)

- using close observation of individual children as the starting point for supporting their developing positive self-concept and their learning (Drummond, 1993).

About dispositions ...

I have referred to the likely characteristics – or dispositions – of effective learners. However there is one disposition that supersedes all of those individual characteristics – *the overall disposition to go on learning.*

The disposition to go on learning depends on a combination of factors:

- Good timing for the teaching and learning of knowledge and skills. This depends on close observation of individual children

- Opportunities to strengthen dispositions (such as the disposition to investigate), and to focus on desirable dispositions, such as accepting peers from diverse backgrounds

- Learning for its own sake, avoiding the danger of the child becoming preoccupied with the judgements of others

- Lastly, the importance of modelling by 'significant adults'. Do we make our own intellectual dispositions – to investigate, ask questions etc. – obvious to children? Do they see us regularly communicating? Asking questions? Learning from our mistakes?

About the context provided for children's learning ...

An intention to implement these four factors raises certain fundamental questions about the context provided for children's learning:

- Are there opportunities and strategies for observing children closely?

- Does the provision facilitate the development of children's cognitive dispositions, e.g. to investigate, question, make choices?

- By what criteria are children's efforts and achievements judged, and by whom? Are children encouraged to make their own judgements about how they are doing?

- How varied are the situations and circumstances in which children can experience adults as positive role models in relation to intellectual dispositions? Are they likely, for instance, to observe adults engaged in genuinely exploring, concentrating, problem-solving?

These are challenging questions for any setting, and are likely to require constant monitoring and review. The disposition to carry on learning must surely be one of the most fundamental – and currently most unconsidered – goals of education.

About setting limits ...

Quite apart from the requirements of daily living, children need some external controls to enable them to proceed with the work of establishing internal ones. It is unlikely that 'out-of-control' children will be feeling good about themselves. Being out of control is a frightening experience and certainly not one that engenders self-respect and confidence. Young children need some external 'scaffolding' to enable them to build up their internalised 'rules' in a positive way. Such controls should be seen as temporary by adults – as a means to an end – but they are very important. Children feel safe when adults are consistently firm as well as accepting and understanding. While saying 'yes' as often as possible, it is also helpful to say 'no' clearly and firmly when it matters.

About schemas ...

Recognising and using children's schemas – developing patterns of repeatable behaviour – can support the self-esteem of children who might otherwise be at loggerheads with their 'important adults' because of their apparently obstinate insistence on playing in certain ways. Acknowledging and making provision for these 'play patterns' is a useful and effective strategy. Easily identifiable examples of schemas and associated objects and activities are:

- connection (joining things together – lego, train track, sellotape)

- enveloping and enclosure (covering things up and putting things inside other things – boxes and bags, envelopes, parcels)

- rotation (circular rotating objects – wheels, balls, 'round and round' chasing games, more formal circle games)

- trajectory (things that move (shoot!) in a trajectory such as footballs, aeroplanes, running water, and games involving running, throwing, kicking, jumping and bouncing)

- transporting (moving things from one place to another – shopping bags, buggies, trailers)

Information on this fascinating subject can be found in the work of Athey (1990), Bruce (1997) and Nutbrown (1994). Working in this way recognises and values children's fundamental interests and needs. Instead of children sometimes experiencing disapproval for playing in ways that are natural and important to them, their self-esteem is allowed to grow. They feel understood and accepted, and encouraged to extend their knowledge and understanding about the things that interest them most.

About partnership between practitioners and parents ...

A child's identity is inextricably bound up with parents and family. To recognise and value a child's family is a confirming way of recognising and valuing that child. Not to do so would be actively to militate against those feelings of safety and acceptance that feed a child's personal and social growth and capacity to learn. This is quite apart from the obvious advantages of the mutual sharing of information, strategies, successes, challenges and support that is the fabric of good home-school partnerships between parents and carers, and early childhood education staff.

It is important for children to know that their important adults are trying to understand and accept one another' perceptions, values and priorities – at least in relation to the thing they have in common, the child. Children living with adults who are determined to respect and communicate with each other are likely to learn to do the same.

About realistic expectations ...

Holding high expectations of children is generally thought to have a powerful positive effect on their learning. Most children thrive on the acceptance and approval of their parents and teachers, and will try to meet their expectations. Sometimes however, external standards may be adopted, or comparisons made with other children, without taking developmental factors in to account. This can result in inappropriately high expectations, which most children find overwhelming and which is liable to generate a sense or fear of failure. Children's ability to maintain confidence and self-respect and to learn effectively can be seriously undermined by inappropriately high expectations.

On the other hand it is possible to be so acutely aware of this danger that expectations are pitched disastrously low. Praise may be offered constantly and indiscriminately, rather than for real effort and achievement. Children may not be challenged to develop real knowledge, understanding and skills about things that they can nearly do; and might develop an inflated idea of their own ability and potential which becomes a major obstacle to their progress. The inner core of realistic self-confidence based on actual achievements which enables them to accept support and criticism – and use it positively – cannot develop. Watching and listening to children must form the basis of our expectations of them.

■ Practical implications

Practical implications for supporting and developing these aspects of the personal and social curriculum can be considered in three areas:

- planning and provision (preparation of appropriate experiences)

- interaction and modelling (adults and their role)

- observation, reflection and discussion (reviewing outcomes)

A grid combining these three areas with the four aspects of the personal and social curriculum can be used as a planning tool to help establish strategies (see page 166).

What sort of items might be appropriate content for such a grid? In early childhood education settings, some stages, situations and activities tend to be particularly rich – or vulnerable – to this sort of learning. The last set of starting points highlights these.

■ Starting points

About transitions: starting at nursery, playgroup or school ...

How important are the very first months and years for laying the foundations of personal and social development?

Children's experiences on entering a new setting are likely to affect their feelings of self-confidence and worth, especially if the new setting is their first

Areas of the Personal and Social Curriculum	Planning and Provision (preparation)	Interaction and Modelling (adults' roles)	Observation Reflection (outcomes)
Perception of Self			
Relationship with Others			
Response to Environment			
Emotions + Learning Dispositions			

step outside the home. 'Will they want me? Will they like me? Will I matter to them?' It may be worth considering the messages that children and their families receive about how much they are valued as indicated by the starting arrangements and how they are welcomed. When the answers to 'Will they want me?' etc. are positive, the children will have learned some important things not only about their own worth but also about how they were made to feel wanted and welcomed, and how they can help others to feel the same.

This is the best time for parents and staff to get to know each other, because the more that staff can know about each individual child, the better able they will be to meet that child's needs, right from the first day. And there is another reason. The first significant contact between parents and staff is often when something has gone wrong and the child is in some sort of trouble and although this usually makes a conversation between staff and parents necessary, it can be difficult to have a genuinely useful discussion if a positive relationship has not already been formed on the basis of knowing what the child has learned at home and *can already do*. In any case, inviting parents to provide information about their children's knowledge, understanding and skills is a good way of recognising and valuing the vital and challenging role that every parent has. This is likely to enhance parents' sense of identity and worth in relation to their children, as well as confirming to children how much they and their families matter to staff.

The development and maintenance of this early relationship is made easier where there is some sort of 'key worker' system. Then every child and parent will know who their own 'special' adult is – the adult they turn to first, talk to most, who knows the important information about their family, keeps the records and makes sure all is well. As early education and care staff tend to work in teams, this system ensures that children and families can approach the special person they need at the same time as having more general contact with other adults in the setting.

About supporting parents in their role ...

How can parents be supported in their crucial role at this stage?

The process of children's personal and social development can be challenging for parents. Sometimes relationships seem to be going well but inevitably there will be difficult periods, often characterised by problems relating to eating or sleeping and the likelihood of tantrums. Behaviour management can become a major issue, especially when children are probably spending an increasing amount of time outside the home, where challenging behaviour becomes even more difficult for parents to deal with. Most parents welcome support with these issues. However the form in which they would like to receive that support varies enormously, ranging from access to sensitive and informative written information (suitable material is available from various organisations, see end of chapter for information), to group sessions or one-to-one situations where parenting issues can be shared and discussed. When thinking about offering this sort of support to parents a range of issues should be taken into account, such as confidentiality, times, venues, parents' access, appropriate staff, source materials, funding etc.

About provision ...

What sort of experiences do children need in order to develop 'confidence, appropriate self-respect and ...... effective relationships'?

Here are some strategies to consider in terms of general provision:

- Opportunities for children to explore, develop and practise **independence** through making choices, taking responsibility, working towards self-discipline

- An environment in which children's **exploration, talk and play** are the primary ways in which they learn

- A setting which constantly seeks to maximise opportunities for **interactions** between children, and between children and adults

- Provision which acknowledges and uses children's **schemas** (play patterns) as a crucially important element in the learning environment

- Adults who perceive children as 'half full' rather than 'half empty', emphasising what they can nearly do as the **starting point** for learning.

Settings which are characterised by these strategies are likely to have excellent outcomes in personal and social education.

About circle times ...

How can children's sensitivity to others be encouraged to grow and develop?

In most early childhood education settings the majority of children's time is spent in play, but at some stage in a session all or some of the children may come together, possibly for songs, rhymes and stories. A small gathering like this can be a good time for discussions, when children regularly talk and listen to each other as well as to the adult. It is an opportunity for reviewing and valuing efforts and progress, and for discussing shared experiences and representations of experiences (play, pictures, models etc.). It can also be used for planning future activities together, as well as for a variety of turn-taking and sharing games. This is the time when children and adults can talk together about many of the issues that arise in relation to personal and social development. Although these discussions can arise at any moment in the day, it is important to plan for and allocate time for them. Groups need to be kept small – no more than ten children. Where a key-worker system is in operation it is easier to make such arrangements. Discussions between a key worker and his/her group of children generally work very well.

About days out and new experiences ...

What can be done to nurture children's disposition to learn? In today's world, how can children's feelings of wonder be nurtured?

Going out can be a wonderful way for children to learn more about themselves and others around them. The organisational challenges can be daunting, but it is almost always worth it – and going out does not have to be a major expedition. Simply walking once around the block or popping into the local shop can give children an enormous amount to observe, think about, discuss, represent, and incorporate into their play.

A standard parent permission form for these little expeditions is advisable. It allows for spontaneity and flexibility – and it is crucial to address issues of organisation and safety. Whether the expedition is major or modest, so many of the aspects of the personal and social curriculum (confidence, exploring new learning, independence, showing respect, taking turns and sharing, responding appropriately to experiences, etc.) seem to thrive in 'going out' situations.

About cooking and eating ...

What is the adults' role in this process (personal and social development), and how do young children learn about the values of their important adults?

This chapter would be incomplete without a reference to the fundamental human activities of cooking and eating. Most children love cooking, especially when they have been involved in deciding the menu. The same applies to eating, whether it is daily lunch-time or a snack of special biscuits warm from the oven. Cooking features high on the list of activities for developing language, maths and science, and taking part in these daily life activities in a small group can enhance feelings of belonging, confidence and competence. In addition, any adult who cooks regularly with children will know how much concentration, perseverance, problem-solving, turn-taking and sharing is likely to be involved. All these elements contribute to the complex factor of children's learning dispositions.

School lunches tend to be a challenge in any setting, and organisation and timing must sometimes take priority. But eating together can be rich with opportunities for personal and social education. Setting up cooking and eating activities carefully in small groups gives adults the opportunity to talk with children in a relaxed and informal way about really important issues relating, for instance, to values. The comparatively long time involved, and the smaller numbers of children likely to be gathered together (in the case of lunch-times, seating arrangements are crucial) means that these discussions can happen quite naturally – around the equivalent of the kitchen table!

More about transitions: moving on ...

What will help children to be independent, to remain eager to explore new learning and to develop the ability to initiate ideas and solve practical problems?

A difficult concept for young children to grasp is that in order to move on to a new place you have to leave the old one. We see this every time children finish playing with something but cannot bear anyone else to have it. It also happens that children can get used to the idea of going 'up' to their next education setting without ever thinking about the fact that this means leaving the current one. For some children, it is this loss of familiar places and people that generates problems in the new place, rather than difficulties relating to the new.

Practitioners can help by acknowledging that when children are leaving to start somewhere new it means that they will not be coming any more. Children – like the rest of us – need to feel that the move they are about to make will be appropriate and manageable. To establish this is absolutely vital. But they also need to know that they will be missed and remembered, and welcomed back if they visit. Often these 'for-old-times'-sake' visits never happen as they may be impractical or the child does not need them, but it can be very helpful to establish the possibility. It is one way to ensure that children's feelings of worth and achievement are supported.

Another element in moving on depends on how practitioners document and report each child's progress and achievements, both to the parents and carers, and to the new setting or school. The issues about parents sharing children's achievements with staff on entry to a pre-school setting apply again as they leave to enter school. This time, both the family and the pre-school setting can provide information about strengths, achievements and needs to the child's new 'significant people'. One useful way of doing this is to arrange for the *parents* to hold the child's record and pass it on to the school. Simply using such a system successfully signals a recognition of parents' crucial role. It goes a long way towards recognising the everyday, all-day nature of much of young children's learning wherever they are, especially in the personal and social curriculum.

■ In conclusion ...

Most readers will be familiar with the DfEE's Desirable Outcomes for Personal and Social Development (1996). Here is a slightly re-ordered and expanded version, with the DfEE elements in bold print.

- *When adults and peers like children's ideas and follow their lead, they will* **be confident.**

- *When children are warmly accepted as important people in their own world, that will* **show appropriate self-respect.**

- *When other people are willing to listen to them and take them seriously, children* **are able to establish effective relationships with other children and with adults, and to work as part of a group.**

- *When adults hold appropriate expectations of individual children based on careful observation the children learn to* **work independently, to concentrate and persevere in their learning, to show the ability to initiate ideas and to solve practical problems.**

- *When children are given responsibility for making choices and for themselves, they* **demonstrate independence in selecting an activity or resources and in dressing and personal hygiene.**

- *When children know that they can trust people to be concerned about their feelings and needs, they* **are sensitive to the needs and feelings of others, and they take turns and share fairly.**

- *When 'important adults' acknowledge and appreciate each child for who they are, children learn to* **show respect for people of other cultures and beliefs.**

- *When children are well cared for and their own property and environment is respected, they* **learn to treat living things, property and their environment with care and concern.**

- *When adults enjoy being with children and share their own responses to a range of shared experiences and events, children feel 'enjoyed' and can* **respond to relevant cultural and religious events and show a range of feelings such as wonder, joy or sorrow.**

- *When children experience time and time again that the important people in their lives take time for them – to listen, to explain things, to let friendship flourish, they* **express their feelings and behave in appropriate ways, developing an understanding of what is right, what is wrong and why.**

It is generally agreed that this list of strategies and outcomes is indeed highly desirable. However perhaps we should ask ourselves why we think it appropriate to expect children of 3 to 6 years to behave in ways not often consistently found in adult life. The list highlights three things very clearly.

Firstly, high quality early childhood care and education affords crucial opportunities to invest in a more civilised society. Secondly, staff working in early childhood care and education need to be of the highest calibre not only intellectually, as indicated by other chapters in this book, but also in terms of personal and social qualities and integrity. Thirdly, if staff of this calibre are to be recruited and retained, there needs to be a fundamental review of recruitment procedures, career structure, and initial and inservice training for early years educators.

In the UK, the status of practitioners in early childhood education and care has been lamentably low. Recognising the vital importance of this work with young children will be essential in shaping a society fit for the challenges of the twenty-first century.

KEY ORGANISATIONS

Community Insight
The Pembroke Centre, Cheney Manor
Swindon, SN2 2PQ
tel: 01793 512612

Development Education Centre
Selly Oak Colleges
Bristol Road, Birmingham B29 6LE
tel: 0121 472 3255

National Children's Bureau
8 Wakely St
London EC1V 7QE
tel: 0171 843 6000

National Early Years Network
77 Holloway Road
London N7 8JZ
tel: 0171 607 9573

OXFAM Education Department
274 Banbury Road
Oxford OX2 7DZ
tel: 01865 311311

Religious Society of Friends (Quakers)
Quaker Social Responsibility and Education Department
Friends House, Euston Road
London NW1 2BJ
tel: 0171 387 3601

Save the Children
17 Grove Lane
London SE5 8RD
tel: 0171 703 5400

Smallwood Publishing
The Old Bakery, Charlton House, Dour Street
Dover, Kent CT 16 1ED
tel: 01304 226800

Values Education Council of the UK / VEC
c/o Faculty of Education, University of Central England
Westbourne Road, Edgbaston
Birmingham B15 3TN
tel: 0121 766 6538

Recommended further reading

Barnes, P (ed.) (1995) *Personal, Social and Emotional Development of Children* Oxford: Blackwell.
A comprehensive, well-organised and thoughtful reference book about the personal, social and emotional development of children, ideal for students. Chapters by different authors – each a leader in the field – covers attachment, disturbing behaviour, families, emotion, sense of self, play, and growth and change.

Mc Bratney, S (1994) *Guess How Much I Love You* London: Walker Books.
Discussions with children about abstract concepts such as relationships need practical starting points, and this well-illustrated little story for young children is moving without being sentimental. It is a lovely book to share with individual children or groups, and is good for generating discussions about families and loving people.

Roberts, R (1995) *Self-Esteem and Successful Early Learning* London: Hodder and Stoughton
Jo and Lily's story is used to describe and explain babies' and young children's developing self-concept, their gradually developing ability to manage their feelings and the other people in their world, and how all this impacts on their learning. This is a book for people who live or work with young children and are interested in the relationship between children's feelings and their learning.

Siraj-Blatchford, I (1994) *The Early Years: Laying the Foundations for Racial Equality* Stoke: Trentham Books
This important and accessible book addresses many of the complex and challenging situations that can arise in early years settings. It makes the crucial point that early childhood education provides the opportunity to lay the foundations for racial equality, and contains the building blocks with which this can be done. It enables the reader to reflect on racial difference, and inequality, and contains an extremely helpful, practical section on good practice in addition to covering policies, legislation and training.

References

Athey, C (1990) *Extending Thought In Young Children: A Parent-Teacher Partnership,* London: Paul Chapman

Best, R. (Ed) (1996) *Education, Spirituality and the Whole Child,* London: Cassell

Bruce, T. (2nd Ed.1997) *Early Childhood Education,* London: Hodder and Stoughton

Drummond, M. J. (1993) *Assessing Children's Learning,* London: David Fulton

Dunn, J. (1988) *The beginnings of Social Understanding,* Oxford: Blackwell Publishers

Harris, P.L. (1987) *Children and Emotion: The development of Psychological Understanding,* Oxford: Basil Blackwell

Katz, L. (1993) *Dispositions as Educational Goals,* Urbana: Eric Digest

Katz, L. (1995) *Talks with Teachers of Young Children,* New Jersey: Ablex

Miller, L. (1992) *Understanding Your Baby,* London: Rosendale Press

Nutbrown, C. (1994) *Threads of Thinking: Young Children and the Role of Early Education,* London: Paul Chapman Publishing Ltd

Paley, V.G. (1992) *You Can't Say You Can't Play,* Harvard University Press

Roberts, R. (1995) *Self-Esteem and Successful Early Learning,* London: Hodder and Stoughton: London

SCAA and DfEE (1996) *Desirable Outcomes for Children's Learning on Entering Compulsory, Education* London: DfEE and SCAA

Sylva, K. (1994) 'The Impact of Early Learning on Children's Later Development' in *Start Right: The Importance of Early Learning,* London: RSA

Siraj-Blatchford, I. (1994) *The Early Years: Laying the Foundations for Racial Equality,* Stoke on Trent: Trentham Books

Siraj-Blatchford, John and Iram (Eds.) (1995) *Educating the Whole Child: Cross-curricular skills, themes and dimensions in primary schools,* Buckingham: Open University Press

Index

Adult support 33

Assessment 15-42, 36, 151

    base-line assessment 20

    formative 22

    self-assessment 41

    summative 22, 38

Behaviour 158

Bilingual learners 48-50

Creativity 139-154

Computers and IT 116-120

Cross-curricular themes 7, 137-174, 161

Cultural identity 4-5

Cultural meanings 9

Curriculum

    breadth 7, 24

    continuity 8, 24, 85

    development 3

    developmental 11

    differentiation 7, 24, 34-35, 69, 82

    framework 3-5,

    integration 26-30

    'natural' curriculum 9, 121

    quality 3-14,

    relevance 7, 69

    variety and pace, 7,

Data-handling 65

Design and technology 109-120

Desirable Outcomes 6-7, 46, 67, 127, 139, 170

Early years curriculum group 12

Effective early learning (EEL) project 13

Effective provision of pre-school education (EPPE) project 13

Emotions 161

Equal opportunities 4-6

Evaluation 34, 89, 115, 151

Feelings 158

Groupings 33, 35

Humanities 121-136

Language and literacy 45-59, 71, 84, 146

Learning 8, 10-12, 20, 32, 34, 38,46, 66-67, 80-81, 85, 102, 123-125, 161-164

Maths 61- 76, 146

Numeracy 62-64

Observations 39, 74

    record sheet 19

Oracy 46

Outcomes 35

Parent involvement 8, 22, 88, 128, 164

Personal and social education 155-174

Physical development 93 -107,

Play 10, 46-47, 70, 72-74, 127

Planning 4,15-42, 69, 86, 98-100, 126, 130-132, 166

Quality in diversity (QuiD) project 13

Recording 39-40

Relationships 159-161

Resources 33, 89, 91, 134-5

Rumbold report 4, 10

School improvement 3

Science 77-92, 144

Sense of self 157

Staff

    development 4

    philosophy 4

Start Right report 5

Topic work 26, 128

Zone of proximal development 11